The Radical Team Handbook

HARNESSING THE POWER
OF TEAM LEARNING
FOR BREAKTHROUGH RESULTS

John C. Redding

JOSSEY-BASS
A Wiley Company
San Francisco

Jossey-Bass books and products are available through most bookstores. To contact Jossey-Bass directly, call (888) 378-2537, fax to (800) 605-2665, or visit our website at www.josseybass.com.

Substantial discounts on bulk quantities of Jossey-Bass books are available to corporations, professional associations, and other organizations. For details and discount information, contact the special sales department at Jossey-Bass.

 Printed in the United States of America on acid-free, recycled stock that meets or exceeds the minimum GPO and EPA requirements for recycled paper.

Library of Congress Cataloging-in-Publication Data

Redding, John C.
    The radical team handbook : harnessing the power of team
learning for breakthrough results / John C. Redding. — 1st ed.
        p. cm. — (The Jossey-Bass business & management series)
Includes bibliographical references and index.
    ISBN 0-7879-5161-7
    1. Teams in the workplace. 2. Employees — Training of.
3. Occupational training. 4. Organizational learning. 5. Team
learning approach in education. I. Title. II. Series.
    HD66 .R43   2000
    658.4'036 — dc21   00-009780

FIRST EDITION
HB Printing   10 9 8 7 6 5 4 3 2 1

THE JOSSEY-BASS
BUSINESS & MANAGEMENT SERIES

CONTENTS

PREFACE

Have you ever stepped back and listened to yourself—really heard what you must sound like to others? A few years ago I had such an experience. I was training a group of middle managers to be project team leaders. Within a thirty-minute period, I heard myself invoking just about every management buzzword of recent years. I remember passionately extolling the importance of "thinking out of the box," "breaking the frame," "becoming a systems thinker," and "shifting paradigms." I recall looking at the group and being greeted with stony silence and blank stares. The managers did not seem to understand.

In retrospect it is clear to me that I was the one who did not understand. I did not understand the complex realities they were facing. I did not appreciate the practical considerations involved in producing real, fundamental change. I did not know how hard it really is to think out of the box, break the frame, and shift paradigms.

This book is the result of over five years of work, as I attempted to understand exactly what it takes to apply these concepts with real projects and real project teams. The effort included conducting in-depth field studies of twenty teams in various organizational settings, tracking their projects from beginning to end. It also consisted of hands-on consulting with several leading organizations in an effort to introduce a fundamentally new approach to team-based project management.

The end result is, I hope, a concrete and practical guide for project team members who are faced with tackling projects that are critical to the success of their organizations in the midst of fast-changing business conditions. These projects typically have one or more of the following characteristics:

- Dramatic results, not just incremental improvements, are needed.
- The projects stem from new situations that companies have not faced before.
- Organizations have repeatedly and unsuccessfully tried to solve these problems in the past.

Increasingly, these are the types of projects that project teams are being asked to handle. With projects such as these, a traditional, step-by-step project management approach (gather and analyze information, explore alternatives, choose the best alternative, and so on) will likely not produce the desired results.

So what approach *will* work? I will show that what works is to think of a project as a discovery and learning process—an approach that surfaces and challenges preconceptions and misconceptions that have long been held as givens in organizations.

At the core of the book are three basic concepts: *speed, depth,* and *breadth. Speed* is how fast project teams are able to discover and learn. *Depth* is the degree to which teams are able to deepen their understanding of their projects. *Breadth* is the degree to which teams impact their organizations beyond the original scope of their projects.

I will also show how teams using the radical project team approach consistently produce breakthrough results far exceeding those of comparable teams.

HOW THE BOOK IS STRUCTURED

You should read the book from cover to cover; each chapter builds on the next. After this initial reading, you'll find the book to be a useful, off-the-shelf handbook.

There are eight chapters and a conclusion, as follows: Part One includes four chapters. Chapter One describes the need for the radical team approach, compares radical project teams to traditional project teams, and provides an overview of what is covered in the book. Chapter Two shows how projects can be understood as a learning process and analyzed as a series of learning cycles. Chapter Three introduces three key factors that need to be considered when assessing the effectiveness of radical project teams: speed, depth, and breadth. And Chapter Four shows how radical teams take purposeful and systematic actions to increase the speed, depth, and breadth of team learning.

Part Two includes four chapters, beginning with Chapter Five, which offers concrete guidelines, tools, and techniques for increasing the speed of team learning. Chapter Six describes concrete guidelines, tools, and techniques for increasing the depth of team learning. Chapter Seven offers concrete guidelines, tools, and techniques for increasing the breadth of team learning. Chapter Eight covers the support needed to implement radical project teams in organizations, including the role of leaders, the selection of team members, and the training of project teams.

Finally, the Conclusion (Chapter Nine) looks at the radical team approach from the perspective of individual team members. Not everyone is equally suited to be a member of a radical team. Some people find the process motivating and challenging. Others find it frustrating and confusing. This chapter describes the personal characteristics that are needed to make best use of the radical team approach. It also describes how the radical team process can serve as a catalyst for both professional development and personal growth.

I've sprinkled the book with case studies designed to illustrate specific concepts and techniques. In addition, the application exercises that are found throughout the book serve two purposes. First, you can use them when reading the book cover to cover as a way to relate the book's content to your own experiences with current or past project teams. Second, you can later select specific exercises to use with project teams at key points in projects. There is also a "Quick Guide to Application Exercises" at the end of the book that lists the application exercises and identifies their intended purpose and use. A "Terms Used in This Book" section, also at the end of the book, defines potentially unfamiliar terms.

A NOTE ABOUT ACTION LEARNING PROGRAMS

There are several similarities between the radical project team approach described in this book and action learning programs. Action learning is a form of management development that uses real-world problems and projects as vehicles for professional growth and development. Many leading firms, including Motorola, General Electric, and Honeywell, are using action learning as a core element of their management and executive development programs (Dotlich and Noel, 1998). In fact, several of the specific techniques described in this book are based on similar techniques employed with action learning programs (Rothwell, 1999).

However, there are critical differences between action learning programs and the radical team approach. In action learning, the primary emphasis is on developing high-potential people to lead the organization in the future. As a result action learning often includes structured classroom training to accompany the project work; a learning coach is typically assigned to each team. Another key feature of action learning is that it operates outside the normal business environment. In action learning there is an attempt to create "a parallel universe, one that bears similarities to a given company's work environment but that is also distinct" (Dotlich and Noel, 1998, p. 16).

The types of methods and techniques used in action learning are not meant to be used as a normal way of tackling projects. In contrast, with radical project teams the emphasis is on producing business results in real projects. People development occurs through the process but is not the primary aim. In addition, there is no attempt to create a parallel universe; instead, the goal is to transform the existing universe into one in which prevailing ways of thinking and doing business are routinely challenged and modified to reflect shifting business realities. The radical project team approach will increasingly become the standard way in which organizations will need to tackle their most important strategic challenges.

With these differences noted, if your organization is currently engaged in action learning, you should find a natural fit with the radical project team approach. Both methods share a similar underlying philosophy and have developed in response to the same irrefutable fact: organizations are increasingly encountering business problems for which nobody has the answer, and learning is the only possible solution. As a result your organization should experience a significant head start in attempting to introduce radical project teams, compared to organizations without action learning programs.

ACKNOWLEDGMENTS

Thanks first go to the hundreds of individuals who served as project team members of the dozens of projects that led to the writing of this book. The names of the individuals and their organizations are kept anonymous to allow for full and candid descriptions of their projects. This book is also indebted to Ralph Catalanello, who partnered with me several years ago in writing *Strategic Readiness: The Making of the Learning Organization*. Ralph helped me to see how learning cycles can be practically applied and measured as a means of understanding how change occurs in organizations. Sincere appreciation also goes to those who helped conduct the research studies that led to this book, especially Laurel Jeris. I would also be remiss if I did not acknowledge the strong influence of the theories and research of Chris Argyris.

I would also like to thank those colleagues and graduate students who collaborated on the team learning studies that led to the book, including Laurel Jeris, Michael Moran, Eric McLaren, Sarah May, Jeanne Connolly, Ellen McMahon, Lou Sharp, Daron Sandbergh, and Lucille Coleman. Thanks go also to Professor John Niemi of Northern Illinois University, who helped support and guide the first round of team learning studies.

I also thank Judy O'Neil of Partners for the Learning Organization, who assisted in pulling together several of the case studies described in the book and from whom I have learned a great deal about team learning and action learning over the years. Thanks go as well to Laurel Jeris for providing feedback on an early manuscript. She, in numerous ways, has helped shape the radical team approach.

I also want to thank Susan Williams and Julianna Gustafson of Jossey-Bass Publishers, who have provided valuable guidance throughout this project. Thanks also to Mary Garrett for a superb job of managing the production of this book.

Finally, I am indebted to the continuous support of Annette Kamm and Richard Kamm, who were with the project from the beginning to the end, who provided thoughtful feedback and coaching, and who have sweated out the many details of getting a book like this finished. I could not have written it without them.

Naperville, Illinois   John C. Redding
July 2000

ABOUT THE AUTHOR

John C. Redding is executive director of the Institute for Strategic Learning (ISL). ISL is a consulting and applied research firm that specializes in the use of organizational learning principles to accelerate high-speed change and achieve breakthrough results. Under his leadership, ISL has partnered with many leading organizations to pioneer innovative methods of strategic planning, project management, and leadership development. He is the author of *Strategic Readiness: The Making of the Learning Organization* (1994, with Ralph Catalanello) and dozens of articles on strategic planning and organizational change.

Redding received his doctorate from Northern Illinois University, where his doctoral dissertation on the interrelationship of strategic planning and human resources received the prestigious Dissertation of the Year award from the American Society for Training and Development. He has taught organizational change and management at Northern Illinois University, Benedictine University, and DePaul University. He is currently chair of the American Society for Training and Development Research-to-Practice Committee. Redding can be reached via the website http://www.radicalteams.com or by e-mail at jredding@islconsulting.com.

The Radical
Team Approach

Radical Teams
An Introduction

chapter
ONE

Radical simply means "grasping things at the root."

Angela Davis[1]

L et me make a guess. You are currently (or soon will be) a member of a team tackling a project like one of the following:

- Your project requires you to produce huge leaps in business performance, not just incremental improvements.
- Your project involves a new situation no one has encountered before.
- Your company has unsuccessfully tried to deal with the situation or problem in the past (maybe several times).
- The success of your project will have a direct influence on your firm's overall business performance and future viability.

  Here are some concrete examples:

- Increasing margin contributions by 25 percent over the next three years while continuing to grow market share.
- Tripling sales over a six-year period without acquisitions.

3

- Becoming a truly international company, offering products and services around the globe.
- Forming a centralized information systems function among four highly decentralized business units.
- Bringing a revolutionary new product to market.

These are all mission-critical projects. They deal with issues fundamental to the competitive positioning of the company in the face of shifting business conditions. Through these projects, companies seek to discover how they can respond to new business realities such as operating as a truly global business, maintaining profitability in the face of intense price competition, keeping up with technological advances, and meeting the increasingly distinct needs of differing market segments.

This book tells the stories of several projects such as these. The most successful increased their firm's competitive positioning amid major changes in business conditions, including the following:

- The distribution arm of a U.S.-based equipment manufacturer had an apparently simple choice to make: consolidate Canadian and U.S. operations or get out of the Canadian market. It was becoming too expensive to run two essentially separate companies. The firm formed three project teams to plan and implement the consolidation of all U.S.-Canadian operations within six months. One project team challenged the consolidation decision, uncovering increasing evidence that full integration would significantly reduce sales, profits, and customer satisfaction in Canada. Instead, it proposed an alternative: integrate operations in a way that would not be noticed by Canadian customers but would still achieve most of the needed cost reductions. Now, several years later, the company has achieved almost all of its cost reduction targets and has increased both sales and profits in Canada.

- A publishing company had been losing customers steadily for several years, supposedly because of poor customer service. The organization engaged several top consulting firms to tackle the customer service issue. However, their recommendations did not help. A project team took another look at the problem, suspecting that the customer service issue might be a symptom of a deeper, more pervasive issue. The team's discovery? The company's product line was obsolete.

- A large public utility facing deregulation knew a simple fact: they had to reduce costs by half or go out of business. But how could this be done? Both labor and material costs were fixed at much higher levels than their new competitors' costs. All obvious cost reduction steps seemed to have been taken. After considerable struggling, a project team came to understand that they themselves, as middle managers, were the problem. There were obvious ways to reduce costs, but they would require new relationships with the workforce and new ways of managing the business. The team exceeded its cost reduction targets. Many of the team's ideas are now being implemented corporationwide.

I contend in this book that a fundamentally new and different form of teamwork is needed to deal with such projects—an approach that is based on learning. In each of the success stories I just described, the project teams did not accept the way the project was first defined. They challenged preconceived notions of what had to be done. They went out and created new understandings of what the project was all about and what had to be done.

A TALE OF TWO TEAMS

A few years ago I had an experience that changed the way I look at project teams. It happened over the course of a single day. I spent the morning working with a project team in a large, global, high-technology organization and the afternoon with a team in a small, local manufacturing company. The two teams were polar opposites.

The "morning" project team was as sophisticated as they get. Team members were highly skilled middle managers who had been recruited from leading graduate business programs. Most team members had benefited from the best that was available in executive and management training. The surroundings were elegant: a cherry-paneled boardroom in the company's high-tech corporate conference center.

The team meeting was well planned and executed. The team quickly walked through the agenda, which had been circulated several days in advance. The team then reviewed the status of the project plan; it was exhibited in a multicolor time line, projected from a laptop computer. The team was on schedule, if not a little ahead of schedule.

The team's project was a high-profile initiative. They were to form a strategic-term alliance with the company's number-one customer—a large retail chain—to sell product directly to the customer and bypass distributors. Direct sales had never been done in this industry. The potential benefits were huge: being able to offer the customer high-speed delivery on a unique product at a cost lower than anything else on the market. If successful, both the company and the customer would realize huge gains.

During the meeting the team was challenged to make a quick decision. The customer had approached the company with an interesting offer: to accelerate the previously agreed-to time line for beginning the direct shipment program. Rather than wait a year, until the annual new-product line would be launched, the customer proposed that a pilot program begin in the current year. Direct shipping of product would need to begin in just three months. The team was intrigued by the proposal and impressed by the customer's aggressiveness. The team displayed the time line chart again. Using critical path analysis, the team looked for possible ways to accelerate the schedule. The team also conducted a systematic risk analysis, carefully weighing the pros and cons of the pilot program proposal. After a few hours of careful review, the team decided that it was too risky to move ahead on the pilot project. The team would recommend that the company decline the customer's proposal and stick to the original time line.

As I drove from one company to the next over lunch, I thought about how well the morning meeting had gone. The team was obviously on top of its project. It had thought out the decision logically and carefully, reaching a consensus that everyone could support. The team seemed the epitome of effective project management and teamwork. People expressed differences of opinion without implying criticism of others. There appeared to be a climate of genuine trust and camaraderie among team members. However, I could not avoid being a little disappointed that the team had not decided to take advantage of the opportunity that the customer had offered them. Here was a chance to get a jump on the competition. The project was ambitious and risky. Yet in my view the risks seemed worth taking.

The "afternoon" project team was a different story. If the morning group was sophisticated and professional, this group was down-to-earth and undisciplined. Most were hands-on manufacturing people: production supervisors, machine operators, and production schedulers. Only a few had completed college. I doubt if anybody on the team had participated in any formal training related to project management or effective teamwork. The meeting occurred in a cramped lunchroom. Bread crumbs and banana peels remained from lunch.

The team had been formed six months earlier to recommend whether the company should introduce a low-cost, off-the-shelf product line. Such a decision would represent a major shift in company direction. The company was a leader in producing high-end, customized products for a niche segment of the consumer goods industry. When it came to business, it was either feast or famine. Orders tended to be huge. A single order could tap out the company's production capacity for months on end. When the order was shipped, the company would be virtually idle until the next big order came. This feast-or-famine pattern had worked fine in the past because of the high margins the company was able to charge. However, that was no longer the case. Cost competition was driving prices down. Entering the low-end market had its advantages: it evened out production demands throughout the year and reduced costs by standardizing production methods.

Boy, was this meeting different from the morning meeting! There was no agenda and no project plan. The team seemed stuck. It was firmly entrenched into two camps, one advocating entry into the low-end market and one against it. It was a classic division between old-time employees and new hires who saw the old-timers as resistant to change. With the president putting on pressure for the team to deliver its recommendations, emotions were high and each side had lost tolerance for the other. People interrupted each other in mid-sentence. Cheap shots and thinly veiled name calling were commonplace. About two hours into the meeting, six months of frustration came to a head. One of the most vocal advocates for the low-end market stood up, obviously angry and upset, and announced that he was leaving the meeting; he hinted that he might even quit, frustrated by the team's unwillingness to come to what he felt was the only logical decision. "I have better things to do than sit in here all day," he said as he left the room. "When the company goes out of business, I'll start my own company and hire people who aren't stuck in the past."

The group seemed stunned and not sure what to do next. Was this the end of the project? What would the team tell the president? Would it report that it was unable to come up with a recommendation? In an apparent attempt to deal with the awkwardness of the situation, the team started casually talking about the advantages of starting a company from scratch to go after the low-end market. They explored some creative ways to streamline production. They identified ways to standardize the product line. They even talked about how the company could be structured so as to keep costs down. The discussion became more and more serious. There was obvious excitement. By the end of the meeting, the team had begun talking about forming a "company within the company"—a separate business unit essentially operating as a stand-alone company outside the existing manufacturing structure. Two weeks later the team met again (including the person who had walked out of the previous meeting). Within six months, the "new company" was launched. The first few orders were pretty tough going, but over time the problems were ironed out. Today, several years later, the new company represents 40 percent of the overall company's total sales, and, even more important, profitability has been restored to an acceptable level.

Since my experience with the two teams that day, I have frequently thought about what happened. Obviously, the morning team was much more highly skilled and professional. The afternoon team embodied much of what is bad and frustrating about teams: inefficiency and personal conflict. Yet when I compared the results produced by the two teams I had to be honest. The morning team had kept business as usual. The afternoon team had transformed its company.

I am not suggesting that the afternoon team should serve as a model for effective project teams. The undisciplined nature of the team has its obvious downsides, including wasted time, destructive effects on personal relationships, and hit-or-miss results. However, my experience that day raised two key questions:

1. Was there something about how the morning team approached its project that discouraged the team from being open to innovative ideas, experimenting, and taking risks?

2. Underlying the apparent chaos of the afternoon team, was something valuable going on? Did the inherent messiness of the approach, the frequent impasses, and the tension among members help stimulate a novel, innovative business solution and a commitment to make it happen?

My personal experiences with the two teams that day have been subsequently reinforced through an experimental research study conducted by Laurel Jeris (1997). Jeris formed eighty, five-person teams, randomly assigning individuals to each team. The teams had not worked together previously. They were given several brief problem-solving exercises similar to the types of real problems many project teams face today. For each exercise, the teams were provided with background information comparable to the initial information often available to project teams. The teams had some hard, concrete data to work from; however, the information was incomplete and ambiguous. Speculations, assumptions, and hunches were thrown into the mix as well. It was up to the teams to develop their best recommendations regarding how the situations should be handled.

One set of teams was guided to act much as the morning team did. When these teams first sat down to work together, they received instructions and coaching in traditionally prescribed teamwork practices. These included agreeing on a logical, step-by-step approach to solving the problems, carefully planning how they would spend their limited time together, and adhering to standard practices of group dynamics ground rules: balanced participation, effective interpersonal communications, active listening, consensus seeking, and respectful conflict management.

Another set of teams, however, was given no help or guidance. They were on their own to figure out how to tackle their assignments and work together. As a result these teams were more like the afternoon team. They often jumped right into solving their problems without coming up with a game plan first. Discussions frequently rambled. Some people dominated and others just sat back. Team members were not always polite to each other.

Most of the teams' recommendations consisted of standard, obvious, run-of-the-mill solutions based on face-value acceptance of the background information. These solutions remained within the "frame" in which the task was originally presented to the teams (Schön, 1983). However, another category of solutions was proposed by some teams. These recommendations were creative and novel. They were based on making careful differentiations between concrete facts and subjective assumptions and hunches. These solutions were the result of a process of reframing the problem that was originally presented. Argyris and Schön refer to this process as "double-loop learning" (1996).

The results of Jeris's experiment backed up my own experiences with the morning and afternoon teams. The teams that were trained to follow traditionally prescribed teamwork practices were less apt to produce novel, creative solutions than the teams that were left to their own devices. In fact, *the teams left on their own were twice as likely to produce novel, frame-breaking solutions* as the teams trained in traditional teamwork practices.

Jeris went a step further. She set up a third group of teams, hoping to harness and capture the positive features of the afternoon team and minimize their unproductive and sometimes destructive characteristics. These teams operated under a set of guidelines that encouraged them to separate facts from assumptions and not to blindly accept the problem as first presented. These guidelines were based on Argyris and Schön's principles of "action science." According to Argyris and Schön (1996), action science creates "conditions for collaborative inquiry in which people . . . function as co-researchers . . . making private attributions public, treating these attributions as disconfirmable, and subjecting them to public test" (p. 50).

This third group of teams produced encouraging results. *These teams reframed their problems three times as often as did the teams that operated using traditional team problem-solving techniques.* This part of the study suggests the possibility of creating a new model of teamwork purposefully designed to increase the likelihood that teams critically reexamine the assumptions with which projects are initially framed and reframe their projects as needed.

THE SEARCH FOR RADICAL TEAMS

This book is the culmination of a five-year search for an alternative to traditional teamwork methods. Numerous colleagues and organizations joined me in the search.[2] Our intention was not to invent intellectually exciting new conceptual models. Nor was it to mount an evangelical campaign to advocate the use of such an approach. From the outset our goal was to be able to describe concretely and practically what teams need to do to put such an approach into action.

As a first step, it seemed like a good idea to have a catchy name for this revolutionary approach to teamwork. The word *radical* immediately jumped to mind. At first I probably liked the word because it clearly communicated the need to produce dramatic transformation, not just piecemeal improvement. Yet, as I soon discovered, *radical* has meanings and connotations that make it an even more attractive and illuminating descriptor of a new approach to teamwork. The word is derived from the Latin term for "root."

> Radical *adj.* 1. Of or pertaining to a root or to roots. 2. Forming the root, basis, or foundation; original, primary. 3. Getting to the root or origin; touching or acting upon what is essential and fundamental. 4. *Math.* Pertaining to or forming the root of a number or quantity; esp. the radical sign $\sqrt{}$, the sign used to indicate that a root of the number to which it is prefixed is to be executed. [Oxford English Dictionary]

When you read the word *radical* throughout this book, think about the word's derivation and its full meaning. Envision the root system of a plant and how what is visible above the surface is a manifestation of complex, unseen forces below the surface. Consider the radical sign ($\sqrt{}$) in mathematics and the analytical method of reducing complex numbers to their numerical foundations. Both of those images capture elements of what is meant by the use of *radical* when applied to project teams. Radical project teams do not accept issues and tasks at their face value. Previously unquestioned assumptions are surfaced and challenged. The real problem is often not what appears on the surface. Only by digging below the surface, getting to the root, do meaning and substantial solutions emerge.

In our search for radical teams, we assumed from the beginning that not all types of problems would require radical teamwork. Traditional teamwork is fine for relatively straightforward projects. But the types of problems we wanted to look at were "wicked" problems, not "tame" problems: "Tame problems allow us to work 'inside the box.' They are manageable; they come with a proper focus, appropriate definitions, and relevant information. . . . Wicked problems, however, come with built-in complexities that make them doubly difficult. Wicked problems present no known algorithms for solution; simply identifying the problem can turn into a major task" (Pacanowsky, 1995, p. 37). Although not all problems are wicked problems, the chaos resulting from rapid change in business conditions is making them increasingly commonplace. As one senior manager recently told me, "I don't see any tame problems any more. And if I did, we would not know what to do with them."

Here is the tricky part: Is it possible to know a wicked problem when you see one? Wicked problems do not always appear like wicked problems at the beginning of projects. The complexity becomes evident only after teams begin digging below the surface. Therefore, it seemed important to set up some fairly objective criteria that could be used at the beginning of projects to determine whether they were likely to turn out to be tame or wicked. We used the following three criteria:

1. *Breakthrough results are required, not just incremental improvements.* In the research and development field the term *radical innovations* has been used to describe products that have one of the following three features: (1) the potential for a five- to ten-times increase in performance compared to anything else on the market, (2) the ability to reduce costs by 30–50 percent, or (3) the introduction of new-to-the-world product features (Rice, O'Connor, Peters, and Morone, 1998). Products such as these are "game-changers," transforming the competitive playing field after

they are introduced. Without using these precise parameters, the same concept can be applied to other types of projects in which major leaps in performance are being required. Here is an example:

> In a low-income elementary school, a team made up of teachers, administrators, and parents is formed to rapidly improve their kids' performance in mathematics. According to standardized tests, fewer than one out of five children is performing at the level he or she should for the grade level.

2. *The project involves a new or unknown situation the organization has not encountered previously and for which no ready answer is available.* Increasingly, firms are being faced with problems or projects they have never faced before. Sometimes, an expert has the answer. Or maybe another organization has figured out what to do. However, in more and more cases, nobody has ever solved this problem. For example:

> A team in a marketing services company seeks to introduce a low-cost, standardized product line to stay competitive. The company has made its money and reputation from being the best at producing high-end, customized, one-of-a-kind products. Everything in the company has been geared toward this end: equipment, staffing, policies, and management styles. Now the firm needs to go in the opposite direction and operate on margins a fraction of what it obtains through its traditional product line.

3. *The organization has tried without success to solve this problem in the past, maybe several times.* This criterion may be the most interesting because the problem itself usually appears to be very tame. All the organization knows is that it keeps going up to bat and striking out.

> A team in a financial services company has tried several times to expand geographically but continues to have problems finding, training, and keeping good staff.

Projects can be wicked problems if they contain only one of these criteria. However, in many cases more than one apply. For example, in the situation of the marketing services company needing to introduce a product line, two criteria are present. Breakthrough results are needed (to operate on low margins, the company must reduce basic product costs by 50 percent), and there has been a history of unsuccessful attempts to accomplish this task.

Using these criteria, twenty projects were selected for study. These projects included the ones just described, as well as the several highlighted at the beginning of this chapter. As shown in Figure 1.1, the types of projects and organizations studied vary widely.

Teams were carefully monitored over the full course of the projects or, for very long projects, through a major project phase that typically lasted three to four months. Records (either written notes or audiotapes) were kept of meetings, documenting key team decisions and actions. In several cases, team members kept personal logs in which they recorded their perceptions of their projects as they were unfolding.

As I describe in Chapter Three, the performance of these twenty teams was evaluated on three dimensions: speed, depth, and breadth.[3]

Evaluation of Speed

Speed refers to the degree to which the teams approached their projects as a process of learning, experimentation, and discovery. With the types of uncertain, wicked problems selected for this study, the underlying premise was that teams would need to develop fundamentally new understandings and solutions. To do so, teams would need to engage in what educator-philosopher John Dewey called a process of inquiry (1938). Through this process, the teams would develop some basic understandings about their projects, plan quick and immediate actions that would verify whether these understandings were correct or not, take the actions, and, based on what they discover, modify their understandings.

As I describe in Chapter Two, entire projects can be looked at as such a learning process, which is often represented as a series of learning cycles (Kolb, 1984; Honey and Mumford, 1995a). Figure 1.2 presents a model of the Team Learning Cycle, as it was used to analyze the work of these teams.

The speed of each team was measured by counting the number of learning cycles completed over the course of its project; the more cycles, the greater the speed of the team's learning. In other words speed refers to learning cycle time.

For example, take two teams that started their projects on the same day and ended their projects on the same day four months later. Let us also say that one team completed ten learning cycles during this period of time, whereas the other team only completed five. The speed of the first team would be greater than the second.

Figure 1.1
Team Profiles

Project Team	Type of Organization	Features — Breakthrough Results Needed	New, Unknown Situation	Past Failures
1. Restructuring	Higher education			X
2. Order Cancellation	Publishing	X		X
3. Performance Management	Manufacturing	X		X
4. Geographic Expansion	Financial services		X	X
5. Fundraising	Higher education	X		
6. Leadership Development	Utility	X		X
7. Staff Empowerment	Utility	X		X
8. Cost Reduction	Utility	X		X
9. Best Practice Dissemination	Utility	X		X
10. Reducing Duplicate Operations	Utility	X		X
11. Writing Improvement	Public school	X		X
12. Mathematics Improvement	Public school	X		X
13. Reading Improvement	Public school	X		X
14. Parent Involvement	Public school	X		X
15. Inventory Management	Marketing services			X
16. Production Scheduling	Marketing services			X
17. New Product Line	Marketing services	X	X	
18. North American Consolidation—Marketing	Manufacturing and distribution	X	X	
19. North American Consolidation—Customer Service	Manufacturing and distribution	X	X	
20. North American Consolidation—Operations	Manufacturing and distribution	X	X	

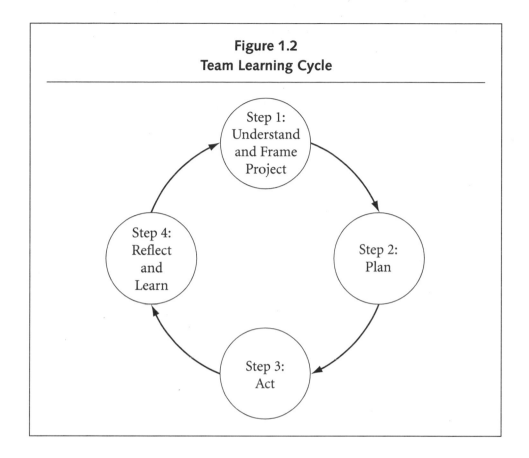

Figure 1.2
Team Learning Cycle

Step 1:
Understand
and Frame
Project

Step 2:
Plan

Step 3:
Act

Step 4:
Reflect
and
Learn

Evaluation of Depth

The twenty teams were also evaluated on the *depth* dimension, that is, the degree to which teams reframe their understandings of their problems over the course of their projects. Evaluation of depth is an attempt to assess the degree to which teams dig deep below the surface of their problems, not accepting the way the tasks might initially appear. Depth represents the ability of teams to develop solutions based on fundamentally new understandings, compared to those that existed initially. Is it always important that teams' conceptions of their projects change over the course of their projects? No. It is possible for teams to confirm that their original conceptions of their projects were correct. However, when facing potentially wicked problems (projects that meet the three criteria listed earlier), teams need to operate under the premise that reframing will be required.

Take the example just cited of the two project teams that started their projects on the same day and ended on the same day. Let us say that one of the teams comes up with a set of recommendations that is based on having developed a whole new way of looking at the project, whereas the second team accepts its problem at face value without going any further. The depth of learning of the first team is greater than the second.

Evaluation of Breadth

The third dimension on which teams were evaluated was *breadth:* the degree to which teams produce results that have a widespread and powerful impact on their whole organization. Breadth reflects the degree to which teams refuse to limit their projects to their original scope and instead seek to influence other projects, other functional areas, other divisions, and maybe the company as a whole. In doing so, teams often affect issues that are critical to the strategic success of the enterprise. In some cases organizations are transformed, maybe for years and years to come, because of the work of individual project teams.

Again, take the example of the two teams that start projects on the same day. Let us say that one team produces recommendations that transform not only the way its own division handles certain issues but the way the whole company does business. In contrast, the other team affects only its own department. The breadth of the first team's learning is greater than that of the other team.

As a result of the speed-depth-breadth assessment, five of the twenty teams listed in Figure 1.1 were selected as most representing the characteristics of radical teams:

- The Order Cancellation Team (team 2)
- The Cost Reduction Team (team 8)
- The Math Improvement Team (team 12)
- The Production Scheduling Team (team 16)
- The North American Consolidation Project Marketing Team (team 18)

As Chapter Three shows, the speed, depth, and breadth of these teams was greater—often much greater—than similar teams with similar projects, often in the same organization. In this book, I refer to these five teams as radical teams. The stories of these teams, as well as several others, are profiled throughout this book.

What did the radical teams do that many other teams did not do? Chapter Four answers this question by detailing a series of concrete action steps that most distinguish the five radical teams from other teams that were studied.

To increase speed the radical teams engaged in the following actions:

- They did not accept projects the way they were originally defined. They avoided any preconceived solutions and, as much as possible, approached projects as blank slates.

- They took special caution to separate assumptions (what they thought they knew) from facts (what they truly knew based on objective information and hard data).

- They took quick and practical actions throughout their projects that were designed to produce the most learning (such as checking out assumptions and finding out things they didn't know).

- They purposefully took actions to accelerate the speed of their learning by reducing learning cycle time.

- They periodically reviewed how well they were learning as teams and took steps to improve their learning throughout their projects.

To increase depth the radical teams did the following:

- They worked to create an environment where it was safe to openly express viewpoints, admit mistakes, challenge each other and the organization, ask for help, and take risks.

- They were sensitive to early warning signs that they might be headed in the wrong direction.

- They openly explored divergent views.

- They exploited breakdowns (frustration, conflict, lack of progress) to produce breakthroughs.

- They purposefully stopped and captured lessons learned at the end of each cycle.

- They were willing and able to reframe their projects to reflect deepening understandings.

To increase breadth the radical teams did the following:

- They were able to uncover connections among seemingly unrelated factors, gradually increasing the scope of their projects to embrace any relevant organizational issues.
- They were proactive in taking actions to influence others in their organizations who could influence project success.
- They purposefully took steps to learn from their organizations' past history in dealing with similar problems.
- They purposefully went against the organizational grain, recognizing that aspects of the corporate culture might need to be challenged to achieve desired results.
- They took responsibility for making things happen elsewhere in their organizations, even when nobody asked them to do so.

The action steps listed were identified by looking at the practices of the five radical teams that provide the basis for Part Two of this book. Chapter Five covers the action steps related to the speed dimension. Chapter Six covers the action steps related to the depth dimension. Chapter Seven covers the action steps related to breadth. Each chapter provides concrete guidelines and practical exercises you can use with your own teams. Chapter Eight highlights the training, coaching, and leadership steps needed by teams seeking to implement these action steps and increase the speed, depth, and breadth of their teams' learning.

RADICAL RESULTS

The ultimate question is this: Do radical teams produce better results than traditional teams? With the sort of wicked problems described earlier, the answer appears to be a strong yes.

Of the five radical teams, all of the teams' recommendations were accepted and implemented. All of the teams produced specific, measurable improvements that met or exceeded the expectations of their organizations. In fact, in several cases their firms now look back and credit the teams with achieving breakthroughs that were critical for the success of the larger organization.

- The Order Cancellation Team (team 2) did more than just solve the order cancellation problem. It was a catalyst in helping the company recognize the need to reinvent its product line and reposition itself in the marketplace. The story of this team is told in the next chapter.

- The Cost Reduction Team (team 8) exceeded the ambitious cost reduction targets by half, lowering costs by 30 percent compared to the goal of 20 percent. More important, the team produced insights into management practices and company-labor relationships that should help the company meet the fiercely competitive challenges caused by deregulation.

- The Mathematics Improvement Team (team 12) produced a 120 percent improvement in the mathematics performance of its students. Within three years, the school moved from being the second lowest to the second highest of the fifteen schools in the district in math performance. The story of the project team and its accomplishment was featured in the local newspaper. Many of the district's other schools have adopted the team's recommendations and have experienced substantial improvements as a result.

- The Production Scheduling Team (team 16) renegotiated its project with the company's president. The team went on to develop an overall restructuring of the company that was designed to make the company customer-responsive and cost-efficient. Initial results show that both are being accomplished. Moreover, the team identified several major changes to organizational culture, company policies, and management practices that are being implemented as well.

- The Marketing Team (team 18) in the North American Consolidation Project changed the company's whole approach to the Canadian market. As a result of the team's work, Canadian sales increased significantly, and operating expenses decreased by half.

In contrast to these five radical teams, six of the remaining fifteen teams never produced recommendations or, if they did, the recommendations were rejected by their organizations. For teams whose recommendations were implemented, the results usually fell far short of desired outcomes. In fact, for most teams it was impossible to pinpoint any measurable outcomes that resulted from their work. In at least three cases, new project teams were quickly formed to take another stab at solving the problems.

A NOTE TO THE READER

This book is intended for use as a practical handbook to introduce the radical team approach with teams in your own organization. You may be serving as a team member, a team leader, or a team sponsor or champion. You may be a senior leader looking into how the radical team approach may help your company deal with rapidly shifting business conditions.

Although the book is meant to be an easy-to-use guide, please read it cover to cover first. The book provides a comprehensive and integrated framework that needs to be understood before anything else makes sense. The first part (the first four chapters, including this chapter) gives you a basic understanding of the radical team approach. You will discover how to look at the work of teams as a learning process (Chapter Two), how to evaluate the speed, depth, and breadth of team learning (Chapter Three), and the concrete actions that separate radical teams from other teams (Chapter Four). The second part (Chapters Five through Eight) shows you how to put the radical team approach into action. It contains numerous guidelines and exercises that you can later pull off the shelf and use as you are working with various teams.

As useful as the book is as a reference, I am convinced that if you understand the overall principles and approaches described in the first half of the book, you'll discover they have just as much practical impact as do the specific exercises in the second half.

Probably the most powerful way to use the book is to share it with other team members and use it as a handbook as you are working through a project. In such a case, everyone might read the first four chapters at the beginning of the project and discuss how the approach might be used to tackle the project at hand. The second half of the book can then be pulled off the shelf and used as needed over the course of the project. There is no better way to learn the radical team approach than with a real team trying to solve a real problem.

A Matter of Learning

You're going to have to come up with a different
way of thinking and doing work.

A sponsor's advice to a team

I have intimate, detailed knowledge of a dozen or so firms: their customers and competition, their past histories and future plans, their strengths and vulnerabilities. For every one of them, fundamental business realities are changing and producing immediate business challenges that go to the core of their missions as businesses. Meeting those challenges will be critical for future viability.

For several of these organizations the challenge is to figure out where and how to compete globally. For others it is discovering how to differentiate themselves to avoid having their products and services become commodities for which low cost is the only competitive advantage. If the game is played on price alone, they know they will lose. Many are struggling with technology issues. They cannot make the same investments their "deep pockets" competitors can, so they have to invest in the right technologies at the right time and ensure that they produce value-added returns. Several are trying to figure out how to deal with increasingly distinct customer segments, each with unique needs. Which segments do they pursue? Which do they let their competitors have?

These are the types of challenges that are increasingly being passed on to project teams to handle. With these types of challenges, dramatic improvements are often required, no ready answers or known solutions exist, and old approaches to solving problems often fail. Here is an example:

Order Cancellation Team

First, a little background about the company: Corporate Publishing Resources (CPR) is a U.S-based printing company that publishes monthly bulletins on various industries. It sells its bulletins on a subscription basis to corporations and other organizations. CPR experienced steady sales growth until the early 1990s, when sales began to flatten out and eventually decline. Several years ago CPR was bought out by a British diversified international publishing and marketing company. Shortly after acquiring CPR, the new parent company mandated that CPR increase its sales and profitability to equal those obtained from the corporation's other markets.

Over the last few years, the company had been struggling with a problem it could not figure out how to fix: extremely high levels of customer order cancellations. Each year the problem became worse, with customers canceling over 170,000 orders during the most recent twelve-month period. Evidence suggested that the problem stemmed from a backlog in order entry. It was taking an average of two months for orders to be entered and for customers to receive a confirmation. The problem seemed to be compounded by the poor customer service that the company's call center provided. Many customers complained that when they tried to call to find out the status of their orders, they were put on hold for long periods of time.

The company made four attempts to solve the problem. In one case the company formed an internal project team that, after three months of study, recommended providing extensive staff training and significantly increasing the number of customer service staff. Both recommendations were implemented, but the problem persisted. In the most recent attempt to solve the problem, the company turned to a top-shelf management consulting firm. The consultants recommended a total reengineering of the order entry process, primarily through new technologies. With high-speed order processing, customers would not have the opportunity to change their minds and cancel orders. However, the company rejected the recommendations as outrageously expensive, calculating the payback to take over fifteen years under best-case projections.

After four failed attempts to solve the problem, the company knew it had to approach the problem differently than it had in the past, and corporate was putting on increasing pressure to get the order cancellations under control as fast as possible. A task force was formed, with people from throughout the company representing various functions and levels. As a first step the task force identified a series of assumptions on which the previous attempts to solve the problem were based:

- That the problem was an internal operations problem related to how customers' orders were processed.

- That customers were canceling orders even though they still wanted to purchase the product.

- That the salesforce had the ability to sell more products if only they would spend more time and effort selling.

- That CPR's products and services were still needed in the marketplace.

Once these assumptions were surfaced, the task force spent a month systematically gathering information that would either support or refute them. For example, task force members talked to the salesforce to find out how orders were actually placed. They interviewed some customers who had canceled orders. They looked at both sales and order cancellation records.

The findings were fascinating:

- A huge percentage of new orders were rebookings from the previous year. That was not the case a few years ago. Since then, the salesforce had been cut from 350 to 150 salespeople; aggressive sales quotas had been introduced for those remaining. Apparently, when facing the pressure to meet sales quotas by certain dates, salespeople were rebooking orders without talking to customers. When customers received written confirmation of the orders, they immediately called customer service and canceled the orders.

- Many customers never wanted to place an order in the first place. Some said they no longer needed regular updates on the industry. Others said they had switched to using Internet-based services that immediately notified them of changes on pre-specified topics.
- The salesforce was making twice as many calls to customers but making fewer sales.

When the team reviewed this information, they recognized that many unstated assumptions were not being supported by the facts. During this discussion one team member proclaimed, "*You know, we're shooting blanks out there.*" This phrase—"We're shooting blanks"—resonated with the team. It seemed to capture what the team had just learned: the company's products were quickly becoming obsolete and noncompetitive. From then on, "We're shooting blanks" became a shorthand way for the team to refer to how it had reframed the problem.

The high number of cancellations was not a customer service problem. It was a strategic product development and marketing problem. Once the problem had been redefined, the team proposed a new set of solutions:

- Conduct immediate and extensive market research.
- Devote expanded effort and energy to fast-cycle product development.
- Explore product diversification and consider expanding to new markets.
- Expand the use of nonprint publishing methods.

In addition the company stopped accepting any rebookings that were not explicitly approved by the customer. Order cancellations dropped to almost zero overnight.

Over the last few years CPR has made a remarkable turnaround. Shortly after this project was completed, the company conducted an extensive analysis of customer needs. Through this research the company began to understand that the market was divided into a series of distinct customer segments. Large corporations—CPR's traditional customer base—were finding less need for a CPR subscription. They could quickly get much more complete information over free Internet sites. Their need was for in-depth staff training programs on the practical impact of specific industry changes. Today, CPR offers a full range of training programs and CD-ROM-based interactive tools. In addition, through its research CPR uncovered a new market segment: the small business–home business owner. In response, CPR established a full SOHO (small office–home office) line of products. At the same time the company began an ambitious acquisition program, purchasing companies that allow CPR to enter attractive new markets quickly. Today, CPR's print-based subscription business has dropped from 80 percent to 45 percent of total revenues. It is again experiencing sales growth of 15–20 percent per year.

Why did the first four attempts to solve the order cancellation problem fail? Efforts had all been based on seeing the problem in the same way, on the premise that order cancellations were being caused by deficiencies in the customer service department. Other framing assumptions existed but were less obvious: that customers still want the company's product, that the best means of disseminating this information is a print medium, and that the salesforce would obtain more sales only if they worked harder. Once these assumptions were accepted, the same set of potential solutions came to mind: provide more training, add staff, redesign how order cancellations are done, automate the process through technology, and others. However, these assumptions were not supported by the facts about what was really going on in the marketplace. Customers could instantly obtain much of the same information from on-line sources that they had been obtaining from CPR's monthly and quarterly publications. New competitors had sprung up to take advantage of the opportunity provided by advanced technology.

The story of the Order Cancellation Team demonstrates two fundamentally different ways to approach projects. Using the first approach, teams accept the preexisting framing assumptions as givens without, in most cases, even being aware they exist. The second openly challenges framing assumptions and reframes the project as a result. The initial attempts to solve the order cancellation problem represent the first approach; the final attempt reflects the second. Using the Order Cancellation Team as an illustration, Figure 2.1 displays the dramatically different results that can occur when projects are reframed.

Figure 2.1
Order Cancellation Project With and Without Reframing

	Order Cancellation Project Without Reframing	Order Cancellation Project With Reframing
Problem	• This is a customer service department problem.	• This is a strategic marketing problem: *"We're shooting blanks out there."*
Framing Assumptions	• This is an internal operations problem related to how customers' orders are processed. • Customers were canceling orders, even though they still wanted to purchase the product. • The salesforce would sell more products if it would spend more time and effort selling. • CPR's products and services are still needed in the marketplace.	• This is a strategic product development and marketing problem. • Most customers never wanted to renew their orders in the first place. • Because of high sales quotas, the salesforce is rebooking orders without asking customers. • The company's products are quickly becoming obsolete and noncompetitive.
Solutions	• Hire more customer service staff. • Train the customer service staff. • Redesign the ordering process. • Introduce new technology.	• Conduct immediate and extensive market research. • Devote expanded effort and energy to fast-cycle product development. • Explore product diversification to new markets. • Investigate nonprint publishing methods.

The case of the Order Cancellation Team illustrates the power of surfacing and challenging framing assumptions. Look at the differences between the solutions produced through these two approaches. Embedded within what was long thought of as an internal operations problem (not processing orders quickly enough and providing poor phone service) was, in fact, a survival-threatening, strategic business issue. Whether this ninety-year-old company would exist in ten, twenty, or ninety years may have been determined by that single moment when the words "We're shooting blanks" were uttered for the first time.

Radical solutions are fundamentally different from traditional solutions to business problems. When framing assumptions are questioned, there is the opportunity to see problems from fresh and eye-opening perspectives, illuminating a new world of possible solutions. The narrow becomes broad. The limited becomes encompassing. Fundamentally new understandings of business realities emerge. For example:

- Problems previously seen as restricted to specific functions are often seen as mere symptoms of pervasive, organizationwide patterns and issues.
- Operational problems related to internal processes are often redefined as strategic issues related to external business conditions.

Organizations are complex systems. Any problem evidenced in any one part of the organization is likely to be intricately entangled with a host of other issues. Organizational problems can often be traced back to multifaceted, deeply rooted causes. The immediate surface problems are presumed to be symptomatic of deeper issues. Searching for systemic solutions can provide fundamental learning for the whole organization, even in the case of narrowly focused change efforts. Such searches often reveal fundamental insights into the basic structures, processes, information systems, procedures, policies, management practices, and norms of the organization.

TACKLING PROBLEMS AS A LEARNING PROCESS

What did the Order Cancellation Team do that allowed it to succeed when other teams had failed? What gave the team the ability to reframe its understanding of the problem? The answer: it tackled the project as a learning process.

Most teams approach projects in a logical, linear fashion. There is a starting point. There is an ending point. And there are the steps along the way. At the beginning of projects, considerable effort is usually spent to define the project and identify desired project outcomes. The aim is to get from "here" to "there" as quickly and efficiently as possible. Projects are typically divided into a series of predefined stages, with each stage to be completed before the next one starts, in a "waterfalling" process (see the "Terms Used" section at the end of the book for an explanation of waterfalling). In many cases teams develop detailed project plans at the beginning of their projects, identifying target dates for completing each stage. In many firms teams are required to present updates on their projects at the end of each stage and receive approval from an oversight group (usually senior managers) to move to the next stage (typically called a stage-gate process). To help them in the projects, teams often rely on planning tools such as Gantt charts, the critical path method, and others.[1]

In contrast, the Order Cancellation Team pursued solutions through an iterative, experiential process of learning and discovery. What are the key differences between the traditional approach to projects and a team learning method?

- According to the traditional approach, a great deal of effort should be spent defining the project at the beginning, and any variations are to be avoided. According to a learning approach, *the way a problem is defined may very well be the problem.* When the original project description is changed, then a whole new range of possibilities opens up.

- According to the traditional approach it is important to map out the project from beginning to end at the outset, creating a detailed road map. In a learning approach *later steps only become clear after some initial steps are completed.*

- According to the traditional approach the scope of projects should be limited within predetermined boundaries. From a learning approach *problems frequently explode from narrowly defined issues to broad, systemic issues that embrace whole organizations.*

- According to the traditional approach unexpected events are to be avoided, and roadblocks are considered impediments. According to a learning approach *unexpected events are sometimes the impetus for breakthroughs, accidents are more important than planned events, and disappointments lead to successes.*

A great deal of evidence is accumulating to support the growing importance of team learning to project success (Parker, 1994). This evidence comes from a wide variety of industries and with a broad range of projects:

- A study of thirty-six large computer manufacturers around the world found that trying to speed up the traditional, step-by-step approach to project management does not get products to market any faster. What does work is a learning-based approach (Eisenhardt and Tabrizi, 1995).

- A study of fifty-six teams in an office equipment manufacturing company discovered that the degree to which teams engage in a learning approach is the number-one factor predicting the teams' overall performance (Edmondson, 1999). The highest-performing teams engaged in high levels of experimentation.

- Revolutionary new products such as Corning's optical fibers and Searle's NutraSweet® were developed through a learning process in which project outcomes and steps are not well defined or predetermined at the outset "but unfold over time as more information is gained" (Lynn, Mazzuca, Morone, and Paulson, 1998, p. 46).

- The use of a software application development method called RAD (rapid application development) that employs an iterative learning approach produces improvements in project team productivity ten times that of traditional methods (Martin, 1989a). In addition, RAD reportedly reduces application development time from eighteen to twenty-four months to an average of three months (Tate, 1998).

- The failure of project teams to learn has contributed to some of the best-known and costly project failures. An example is the Cochlear Implant Project, described in Chapter Six (Garud and Van de Ven, 1992). For years and years the project steering committee held on to its original belief that a single-channel device would be the best product, despite irrefutable evidence to the contrary. By the time the steering committee changed its mind, it was too late. After an investment of tens of millions of dollars the project was stopped; its rights and remaining assets were sold to a competitor.

In a world of rapid change the primary advantage of a learning-based approach is that it increases the speed with which firms can come to grips with new business realities. The purpose is to find out in a few months something they might not otherwise figure out for years and years to come.

So how should teams approach their projects—as straight lines or as iterative cycles? From a traditional project management perspective or from a learning-based perspective? Project teams need to hold both views of their projects at the same time. To the degree that certainty exists, traditional project management is important. To the degree that uncertainty exists, a learning-based approach is important. Both need to be interwoven in an integrated approach to project management.

In recent years many organizations have set up systems to complete project postmortems and identify lessons learned from one project that can be used to improve future projects. However, it is still fairly rare for firms to take a learning approach to projects themselves (Kotnour, 1999). There is probably ample reason why. It sounds like a messy, slow, haphazard, trial-and-error process. How can companies run businesses this way? How can teams be held accountable for results? How can senior management tolerate a process that is so ambiguous? These are all legitimate concerns.

A primary aim of this book is to present a realistic and practical approach to managing team projects as a learning process. To do so, it is important to demystify the fuzzy, ambiguous nature of team learning. It is essential that teams have the capability to manage the team learning processes, much as they have with traditional approaches. That's where the idea of learning cycles comes in.

THE TEAM LEARNING CYCLE

The learning cycle is not a new idea. It derives from educator-philosopher John Dewey's notion of inquiry (1938). According to Dewey the best way to resolve uncertain situations is to engage in a repeated pattern of thinking about problems (identifying what you know and don't know) and then taking practical actions designed to obtain new understanding. The cyclical inquiry process is similar to the process of peeling back the layers of an onion, with each layer representing new understanding that is created through new actions. The learning cycle has been used to describe how people learn through their everyday experiences (Kolb, 1984; Honey and Mumford, 1995a). It has also been employed to show how companies improve the quality of their products and services (Juran, 1988), discover new approaches to their businesses through strategic planning (Redding and Catalanello, 1994), and effectively implement large-scale organizational change (Dixon, 1994).

In much the same way, the entire work of project teams can be understood as a series of learning cycles. Figure 2.2 provides an illustration of the team learning cycle as it is used in this book.

Step 1: Understand and frame the project. In the first step, teams create shared understandings of what they are trying to do and how they are going to do it. At the beginning of projects these understandings are fairly general, mostly consisting of clarifying the purposes, goals, and deliverables of the projects. By the end of the projects these understandings have matured into specific, fact-supported analyses of the key factors or causes, as well as concrete proposals for future action. From

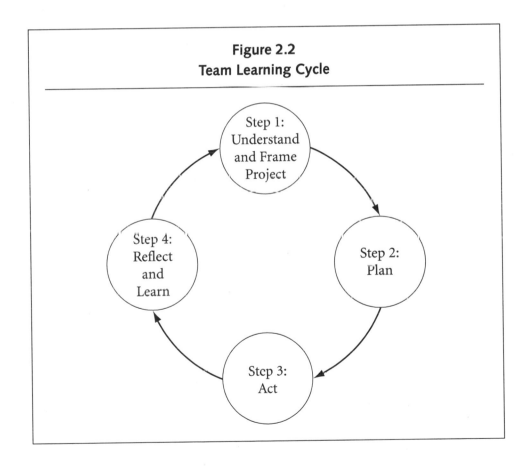

Figure 2.2
Team Learning Cycle

cycle to cycle it is possible to see how much teams have learned by comparing the understandings that exist in Step 1 in one cycle to the understandings that exist in Step 1 of the next cycle. The greater the difference, the more that has been learned.

Step 2: Plan. A learning-driven approach requires teams to plan actions in a different fashion than they might have otherwise. In traditional project management, teams plan actions that will allow them to move as directly and quickly as possible to the completion of their projects. In a learning-driven approach teams plan actions that will allow them to learn as much as possible from cycle to cycle. These actions are purposefully directed toward testing out the validity of framing assumptions. During this process the team plans and takes actions designed to produce learning by answering such questions as these:

- What don't we know that we need to know?

- What actions can we take between now and the next meeting to find out what we need to know?

- How can we verify that what we are assuming is actually true?

Step 3: Act. The key to learning is action. Just as important as what teams do in meetings is what they do between meetings to test out assumptions, to experiment, to gather new information, and to try out hunches. Only by acting do teams have the opportunity to learn.

Step 4: Reflect and learn. This is where the real learning occurs. Now is the time that teams need to be able to slow down, reflect on what has happened, and capture lessons learned. Reflection needs to occur in a spirit of openness and honesty, not in a climate of self-protection or criticism.

Entire projects, from beginning to end, can be understood as a series of learning cycles. Such an analysis might look something like the following. At its first meeting the team examines the task or problem at hand, identifies what it knows and does not know, surfaces some assumptions about the problem, and develops an initial plan of action (such as checking out the assumptions and gathering some additional information). Between meetings, these actions are taken. At the second meeting, the team reflects on what it has learned and draws some conclusions. At this point, the first learning cycle has been completed.

During the second meeting, the team plans some new actions to be taken based on its current understanding of the situation. This plan starts a second learning cycle. Actions are taken between meetings and at the third meeting. Once again, the team reflects on what it has learned and draws conclusions. Over the course of several months, the team engages in numerous learning cycles. Each cycle provides the opportunity for the team to challenge framing assumptions, create new understandings, and find radical solutions to the issue at hand.

In reality the process is often more complex and difficult to detect than just described. Teams do not always begin and end cycles at each meeting. Sometimes teams end meetings without clearly specifying a course of action to be taken before the next meeting. In addition, cycles can occur without requiring formal, face-to-face team meetings. For example, several team members may meet informally, reflect on action that has been taken, and decide, on behalf of the team, to develop a revised plan of action as a result.

THE ORDER CANCELLATION PROJECT
AS A LEARNING PROCESS

Let me illustrate how the story of the Order Cancellation Team can be portrayed as a series of learning cycles. Figure 2.3 presents a drawing of the first learning cycle.

Step 1: Frame and understand the project. The team's sponsor (the vice president of operations) presented the purpose of the project: to develop a set of recommendations within three months that would substantially reduce order cancellations. The team reviewed the background information that it had available regarding the number of order cancellations and the long backlog in entering orders. As did previous teams, the team generally assumed that the order cancellation problem was linked to the long backlog of entering orders in the customer service department.

Step 2: Plan actions. Toward the end of the first meeting, the team identified additional information it would like to obtain before it met again. This included determining from the accounting department the exact number of order cancellations and finding out more from customer service regarding the backlog in entering orders.

Step 3: Act. Between the team's first and second meetings a few team members met with the accounting department. They obtained up-to-date information on the number of cancellations. The year-end figures had just come in, and order cancellations had increased over 50 percent, representing more than $1 million in sales.

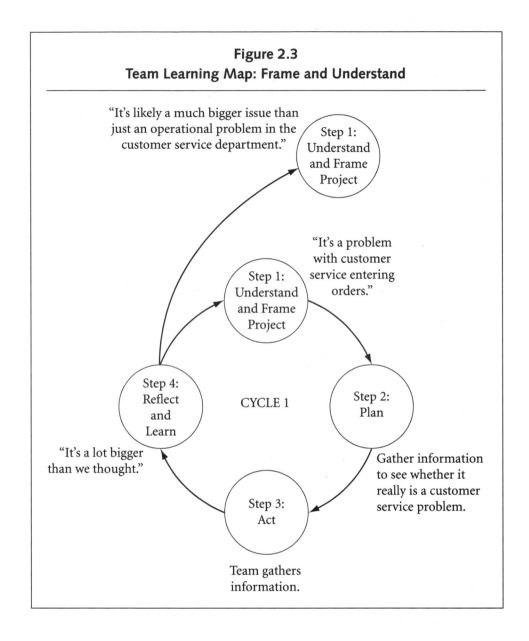

Figure 2.3
Team Learning Map: Frame and Understand

"It's likely a much bigger issue than just an operational problem in the customer service department."

Step 1: Understand and Frame Project

"It's a problem with customer service entering orders."

Step 1: Understand and Frame Project

CYCLE 1

Step 4: Reflect and Learn

Step 2: Plan

"It's a lot bigger than we thought."

Gather information to see whether it really is a customer service problem.

Step 3: Act

Team gathers information.

The accounting department also complained that there appeared to be more and more mistakes with orders: either information was incomplete or it was wrong. This caused problems not just for the accounting department but for customer service and sales, because everyone had to play detective to figure out why customers did not get what they said they had ordered. A few other team members met with the customer service manager, who complained that the whole burden of doing orders had now begun to fall to customer service. In the past the salesforce had written the orders; they had even looked up all product numbers in the company catalogue. Now they might just telephone the order in or write it on a scrap of paper with the bare minimum of information. In addition, the customer service manager reported that several customers had called to cancel orders and complained that their salesperson had started rebooking orders without letting them know.

Step 4: Reflect and learn. At the beginning of the second meeting, the team reviewed the information it had gathered. There was general surprise that the problem was as big as it was and that the number of cancellations had risen so significantly. The meeting went a full hour longer than planned. At several points there were heated exchanges, especially between the salespeople and customer service representatives, each blaming the other for a host of different problems, some related to the order cancellation problem and some unrelated. At the end of the meeting one member tried to summarize where the team was: "Well, I think we can all agree on one thing about the order cancellation problem—it's a lot bigger than we thought." The team agreed to meet again a week later and continue discussing the information and decide what it was going to do next.

Figure 2.4 is a learning cycle map of the entire Order Cancellation Project.

The entire project lasted sixteen weeks from the first meeting until the team made its final recommendations. A total of five cycles were completed during the sixteen-week period.

Cycle 1: In the first cycle, as noted earlier, the team began to find out that the order cancellation problem was caused by more than just a delay in entering orders in customer service. Something bigger was going on.

Cycle 2: In the second cycle the team discovered that when subscriptions were ready to expire, sales representatives sometimes rebooked orders without talking to customers. With the imposition of monthly sales quotas, sales reps generally felt

Figure 2.4
Team Learning: Order Cancellation Project (Complete)

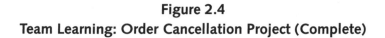

Company needs to take both short-term and long-term actions to solve problem.

Product line is likely noncompetitive and obsolete: "We're shooting blanks out there."

Automatic rebooking is a major cause of order cancellation.

Automatic rebooking may be contributing to the order cancellation problems.

It's a lot bigger than we thought. Other factors are contributing to the problem.

It's a problem with customer service entering orders.

that they did not have the time to talk to every customer when it was time to re-book a subscription. As one sales representative said, "I know my customers, and I wouldn't rebook an order if I knew the customer didn't want it."

Cycle 3: Here the team discovered that most of the order cancellations were from rebooked orders or from orders entered incorrectly. When presented with this information, the team now believed that the problem was being caused in large part by the unsolicited rebooking of customer orders. When customers received confirmations, they cancelled the orders. As one member said, "It's a sales department problem. They're rebooking orders without checking with the customers. Stopping this will immediately reduce order cancellations." Other members disagreed, especially the sales department representative. It was his point that the team had not gotten to the real issue yet. "Why are we losing customers to begin with? Ask anybody in the sales department and they'll tell you, 'We're shooting blanks out there.'"

Cycle 4: After further investigation, including conducting some customer interviews and informal competitive benchmarking, the team eventually came to a joint understanding that the automatic rebooking was a fairly minor issue. A more significant issue became apparent: the company's products were quickly becoming obsolete and noncompetitive. The company was, in fact, shooting blanks out there. However, major controversy remained. Some members felt strongly that the team had overstepped its authority. The team had been asked to look at the order cancellation problem with the assumption that it was being caused, at least in part, by a backlog in entering orders in customer service. Now the team was looking into major strategic issues well beyond its original charge.

Cycle 5: The team decided to meet with its sponsor and present the information it had gathered to determine whether they should continue pursuing the big issues. The sponsor recommended that the team make a presentation to the company's executive committee, in which it would present all information gathered to date and make recommendations to address both the narrow and broad issues. The team began thinking about the project as two-pronged: making short-term and long-term recommendations.

The team then made its recommendations to the executive committee. It began by presenting a flow chart that showed how the presenting problems (order cancellations and order-entry backlogs) were only symptoms of major strategic issues (see Figure 7.3 in Chapter Seven). New competition and technologies had led to flat sales, which in turn led to a corporate sales mandate from the new parent company. This mandate caused pressure for immediate sales increases, which led to both a monthly sales quota per person and an effort to reduce salespeople's time doing paperwork. To accomplish that, the customer service department was assigned more of the order entry, which in turn created an increased workload in customer service and caused a backlog in order entry. The sales quota led to the salesforce automatically rebooking orders, which led to increased order cancellations.

The team then presented its two-pronged set of recommendations. Short-term recommendations included stopping any rebookings that were not explicitly approved by customers and requiring the salesforce to submit completely filled-out order forms. The long-term recommendations, although fairly general, included the following:

- Conduct immediate and extensive market research.
- Devote expanded effort and energy to fast-cycle product development.
- Explore product diversification to new markets.
- Investigate nonprint publishing methods.

The team's recommendations, now several years later, are being credited with serving as the impetus for an organizational renaissance.

The case of the Order Cancellation Team shows how projects can be understood, not as just a step-by-step problem-solving process but as an iterative process of discovery and learning. The next chapter goes a step further. It shows how certain teams are able to harness the power of team learning to produce breakthrough solutions and dramatic results.

Assessing Team Learning

*The team was unlike any of the other teams. It moved fast. It questioned
everything. And, above all else, it made a real difference. If every other
team was like this one, we would have very few problems.*

From an interview with a project champion

In the last chapter I described the first step in the search for radical
teams: looking at team projects as a cyclical learning process. The
next step is to assess the relative effectiveness of multiple teams in various
settings with differing problems, with the hope that certain teams
will stand out from the rest as superior in team learning. If found,
these teams can serve as exemplars of the radical team approach.

With the help of my research team, I studied twenty teams with this in mind.
The projects and organizations appear in Chapter One (see Figure 1.1). We assessed the twenty teams on three factors:

- *Speed:* Did the teams approach their projects through an iterative learning
  process, or did they follow the traditional, linear approach to project
  management?

- *Depth:* Did the teams fundamentally deepen and alter their understandings of their problems over the course of their projects, reframing the projects as a result?

- *Breadth:* Did the teams produce concrete results that had a significant and pervasive impact on their organizations, well beyond the original scope of the projects? In other words were their organizations transformed in some fundamental ways as the result of these project teams?

This chapter presents the results of the assessment of the twenty teams. As expected, certain teams stood out from the pack. Take the example of the three teams that worked on portions of the North American Consolidation Project: the Marketing Team, the Customer Service Team, and the Operations Team. One team—the Marketing Team—was evaluated as clearly superior to the rest on all three factors of team learning: speed, depth, and breadth. Read the following case study, paying special attention to how the Marketing Team approached this project differently than did the other teams.

North American Consolidation Project

A division of a large U.S.-based office equipment manufacturer determined that competitive pressures required that U.S. and Canadian operations be consolidated. The general manager of the division established several teams to develop plans for the consolidation, including a Marketing Team, an Operations Team, and a Customer Service Team. To avoid raising concerns from Canadian employees about possible downsizing, the consolidation would not be announced until later. For the same reason there were no Canadians on the project teams. However, teams were each assigned two sponsors: one from the United States and one from Canada. The Canadian sponsor's job was to provide teams with whatever information they needed to develop consolidation plans for their assigned areas.

To start the project, the three teams attended a two-day project kick-off meeting. The first morning the teams were told about the consolidation and its importance to the business. The three teams were given the same deadline: six weeks to develop general recommendations and six more weeks to develop detailed consolidation plans. After the morning briefing, teams went to individual breakout rooms to develop their project plans. The sponsors were on call if the teams needed help.

Two of the teams experienced no problems in developing their project plans and needed little help from their sponsors. The Marketing Team, however, was different. From the very beginning, the team seemed to be struggling. Several team members raised concerns about the practicality of consolidating Canada and the United States into a single operation. They asked: "Was the expectation that marketing in the United States and in Canada be done the same way?" "Was the company willing to lose sales in Canada?" After a few hours the team called in its sponsors. The sponsors reinforced what was said in the morning: the company was losing money by running two separate operations in the United States and Canada. Something had to be done quickly.

Dissatisfied with the sponsors' responses, the team contacted the division's advertising director to obtain some hard data regarding marketing budgets in the two countries. Team members were surprised by the differences between advertising expenditures in the United States and Canada. In the United States advertising dollars were devoted to a series of large national advertising campaigns, using a combination of television and national print-based media. In Canada the organization relied almost entirely on direct mail marketing. Experience had shown, according to the advertising director, that direct mail seemed to work better. He was not sure when the last time a national advertising campaign had been tried in Canada.

At the end of the two-day kick-off meeting, the other teams presented detailed project plans. However, the Marketing Team had little that was concrete to present. Team members felt they did not know enough about Canada to even begin developing a plan for consolidation. The team suspected that this might be true for the other teams as well. The team recommended that the project be postponed for a short while, that the consolidation be announced, and that Canadian representatives be added to each team. In addition, the team asked if team members could go to Canada and travel with sales representatives for a few days to visit some key customers. The general manager responded that the project would not be postponed. However, he directed the team to work closely with its Canadian sponsor and stated that he was sure the team would be able to get the information it needed. He also saw no problem if team members wanted to travel with Canadian sales representatives and visit some customers, if they felt that the visits were really necessary.

After the two-day kick-off meeting, the teams began working on their projects. The Marketing Team developed a questionnaire that members would use when visiting Canadian customers. A draft questionnaire was pilot tested over the phone with a few Canadian customers. The customers did not want to talk just about marketing issues. They also raised distribution, customer service, and other issues as well. The questionnaire was expanded and revised, based on the pilot interviews.

Over the next few weeks, team members went to Canada for two to three days each, traveling with sales representatives in different parts of the country. The team was surprised at the differences that existed in the various regions of Canada. As one team member put it, "Canada is not one country but a bunch of smaller countries." The customers were different. The product mix was different. The competition was different. The team was convinced that these regional differences explained why direct mail worked so well in Canada. Advertising could be directed specifically to each market segment.

Marketing issues also seemed intertwined with distribution practices. The company ran two central distribution centers, one in Toronto serving central Ontario and one in Quebec. For the rest of the country, the company relied on outside distributors, as it did in the United States. Forty-five percent of Canadian sales and 60 percent of its profits came out of the two distribution centers. The Quebec distribution center also included a French-speaking customer service call center. Each distribution center handled its own direct mail campaign, offering product specials directed toward their customer base and designed to reduce product surpluses. Many customers cited the central distribution–customer service centers as being a primary reason for purchasing from the company. For example, for Quebec customers, having a physical presence in Quebec was important.

Six weeks into the project the three teams met to update the general manager on their progress. The other two teams had completed their projects as planned. They had met once over the six-week period to review the information that had been gathered, develop recommendations, and prepare their updates. Their plans consisted of a total integration of all Canadian operations into U.S. operations. For example, the Distribution Team proposed that the two regional distribution centers be closed and that all customers be served through outside distributors. The Customer Service team similarly recommended that all customer service be provided out of a single, U.S. call center and that French-speaking customer service representatives be hired to service Quebec customers.

In contrast, the Marketing Team recommended that the consolidation be approached with increased sensitivity to the Canadian market and to regional differences. During its update the Marketing Team offered a comprehensive profile of the Canadian market. It divided the country into four sections: the Toronto area, Quebec, the West Coast, and everywhere else. For each section, the team presented sales by product line, market share estimates, types of customers by industry, and advertising expenditures. The team also supplied representative comments from Canadian customers, highlighting their feelings toward a wide range of issues, including distribution and customer service.

The Marketing Team's presentation triggered a lengthy and heated discussion. The members of the other two teams disagreed with the Marketing Team's analysis and resented the team for encroaching on their territories. However, several of the Canada-based sponsors strongly supported what the Marketing Team had said, providing additional evidence from their own experiences. The general manager said very little but encouraged everybody to have an open mind. At the end of the discussion, the general manager announced that he might have been wrong in thinking that a full consolidation of Canadian and U.S. markets made sense. He instructed each team to take another look into its area in light of the information presented by the Marketing Team. A six-week extension would be provided. Rather than consolidating all operations across the board, the teams should look for creative ways to obtain most of the benefits of the consolidation while keeping the consolidation as invisible as possible to Canadian customers. Customers should not feel that their service levels were reduced in any way. He also said that he was now convinced it was important to have a few Canadians on each team, and an immediate announcement of the consolidation would be made to Canadian employees.

Six weeks later than originally targeted, the final consolidation plans were agreed upon. Any operations that were "behind the scenes" and not directly visible to Canadian customers would be integrated into U.S. operations. Both central distribution centers were kept open, although more streamlined than before. Quebec maintained its own customer service call center. All Canadian sales continued to be conducted in Canadian dollars. Despite the fact that Canada retained some separate operations, the consolidation produced about 80 percent of the total cost savings that might have been achieved if all operations had been consolidated.

A year after the consolidation, a customer survey of Canadian customers was conducted. Most customers did not even know that a consolidation had taken place. Moreover, more customers thought that service had improved over the past year than thought service had declined. In addition, Canadian sales had increased at the same time.

Figure 3.1 portrays the work of the Marketing Team during the first six weeks of the consolidation project.

Figure 3.2 shows what the other two teams did during the same six-week period.

The maps reveal considerable differences in the speed, depth, and breadth of team learning of the Marketing Team compared to the other two teams.

Evaluation of Speed

As mentioned earlier, speed refers to the degree that teams approach their tasks as a learning process rather than relying on a purely linear, traditional approach to their projects. To measure the speed dimension, the teams were evaluated based on the number of learning cycles that were completed over the course of their projects. The Marketing Team completed five learning cycles while the other two teams completed two cycles each.

Why should project teams care about speed? The more cycles, the greater the opportunity to learn. However, merely having more cycles does not guarantee that teams will learn. (That is where the depth dimension comes in.) But increased speed does enhance the likelihood that teams will obtain new information and insights that will alter their thinking about their projects.

Initially, assessing the speed of team learning might sound like a purely analytical exercise of counting cycles. However, when you watch teams in action, the difference between high-speed teams and other teams is usually readily apparent. High-speed teams like the Marketing Team bring an experimental spirit of discovery to their projects. They rapidly identify what they know and do not know and engage in quick experiments of discovery (gathering information, finding

Figure 3.1
Team Learning: North American
Consolidation Project—Marketing Team

Full consolidation is not practical.
Any consolidation needs to be
invisible to Canadian customers.

(Step 5)

We need different marketing approaches
for different parts of Canada. Distribution
and customer service also need to be different.

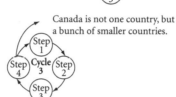

Canada is not one country, but
a bunch of smaller countries.

We need to take a look at a broader
set of issues, not just marketing.

We will fully consolidate Canadian and U.S.
marketing operations. The Canadian market
is much the same as the U.S. market.

Figure 3.2
Team Learning: North American
Consolidation Project—Other Teams

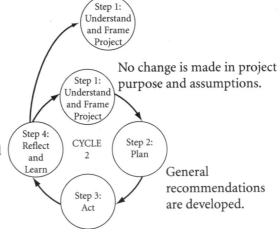

No change is made in
project purpose and assumptions.

No change is made in project
purpose and assumptions.

Team reviewed feedback
from presentation, decided
on needed changes to
recommendations.

General
recommendations
are developed.

Team presented recommendations
and received feedback.

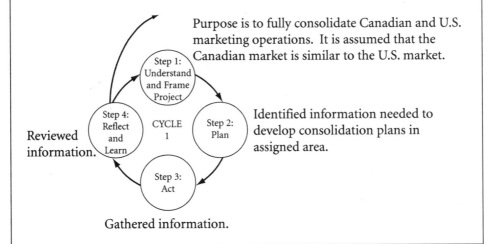

Purpose is to fully consolidate Canadian and U.S.
marketing operations. It is assumed that the
Canadian market is similar to the U.S. market.

Identified information needed to
develop consolidation plans in
assigned area.

Reviewed
information.

Gathered information.

objective data to support or refute assumptions, engaging in experiments, and checking out hunches). Radical teams are humble, recognizing that they do not have the answers and that they can only discover solutions through a learning process.

Evaluation of Depth

Depth refers to the degree to which teams deepen their understandings of their projects from cycle to cycle, challenging framing assumptions and reframing projects as needed. Depth assesses the degree to which teams dig deep below the surface of their projects, not accepting the way problems or tasks might initially appear. Depth is measured by answering the following question: *Was the team's conception of the project at the end any different from what it was at the beginning?*

In the North American Consolidation Project, except for the Marketing Team, the teams did not change their basic understandings of the project from one cycle to the next. Each of the teams accepted the project the way it was originally defined. Never did the teams raise issues regarding such underlying assumptions as

- All U.S. and Canadian operations should be fully consolidated.
- The Canadian and U.S. markets are similar.
- A consolidation will not have a negative impact on Canadian customers.

In contrast, the Marketing Team challenged these assumptions. From cycle to cycle it gradually deepened its understanding of the project. By the end of the two-day kick-off meeting the team had already determined that there were critical differences between the two countries in how advertising dollars were spent. After visits to Canada the team could confirm a wide range in key differences and provide data that the consolidation might hurt customer satisfaction and sales.

Evaluation of Breadth

Breadth refers to the degree to which the learning that occurs within project teams is shared and used by their organizations. If the learning stays within the team, it has little impact. The full impact of the team's learning is only achieved when what has been learned is understood and acted on throughout the organization.

That was certainly the case with the Marketing Team in the North American Consolidation Project. From the beginning of the project, the Marketing Team refused to stay limited to marketing-related issues. Members suspected that complex interconnections existed among a variety of factors. As the project progressed, the team discovered issues related to the work of the other two teams—Customer Service and Operations. By the end of the project, the Marketing Team had changed the company's entire approach to the consolidation and, in all likelihood, the company's overall approach to the Canadian market.

Breadth is a tricky dimension. It might sound as if breadth merely refers to whether teams communicate their insights and conclusions to others in their organizations. There is more to it than that. Radical teams adopt a much different orientation to their projects than do other teams. From the very beginning of their projects, they see themselves as emissaries and agents acting on behalf of their entire firms, not just acting on their own. Radical teams are able to uncover complex interrelationships that exist among a variety of seemingly unrelated factors. Radical teams seek to maximize the impact of their projects on whole organizations. Boundaries do not exist.

So far, I have talked about speed, depth, and breadth as if they are unrelated. In fact, they are highly interrelated. Speed measures the cycle time of the process that produces learning. Depth measures the degree of learning that actually occurs over the course of projects. Breadth measures the overall impact of project team learning on their organizations. One affects others. Increased speed fosters increased depth. As problems continue to persist from one cycle to the next, there is an enhanced likelihood that teams will appreciate the need to get below the surface of projects. Increased depth leads to increased breadth. As more profound learning occurs, the solutions will deal with more systemic issues of organizations. Systemic issues often affect a wide range of organizational issues, thus there is an increased likelihood that the new knowledge will transfer more easily to other issues or business units in the companies.

ASSESSMENT RESULTS

The North American Consolidation Project shows how the speed, depth, and breadth of various project teams can vary widely. The teams in the project were three of the twenty teams we studied in an attempt to systematically assess the speed, depth, and breadth of team learning. All projects met one or more of the three criteria for radical projects described earlier:

- Breakthrough results were required, not just incremental improvements.
- The projects involved new or unknown situations the organization had not encountered previously.
- There had been one or more unsuccessful attempts to complete the task or solve the problem in the past.

Projects spanned periods from two to six months, with the majority lasting between three and four months. In almost all cases an observer knowledgeable in the framework sat in on all team meetings from the beginning to the end. After the projects were completed, the observer was interviewed and a case description of the project was written. For some of the projects, audiotapes and team member logs were also kept and referred to in the creation of the case descriptions. These case descriptions were then used to assess the speed, depth, and breadth of the teams' learning.

The study involved five different "comparison groups," made up of from three to six teams each. Each comparison group consisted of a series of teams that were created at the same time and that operated under the same conditions. In most of the cases they were from the same organization. They received identical training and support. They completed projects that were similar in nature. They had comparable deadlines and deliverables.

Each project was evaluated on the speed, depth, and breadth of the team's learning. For speed, the number of learning cycles was calculated. As can be seen, the number of cycles varied significantly, from a low of zero to a high of seven. For depth, it was determined whether the project—as defined and understood at the beginning—had been substantially reframed by the end of the project. Although all of the projects were selected based on criteria that suggested that reframing might be needed, only seven of the twenty teams actually reframed their projects. For breadth, it was determined whether the project produced demonstrable impact beyond the original project scope. Here, five of the twenty teams were assessed as having broad impact.

From each of the five comparison groups, one team was then selected as the highest-rated team, based on an overall consideration of the speed, depth, and breadth ratings. These teams most represent the radical team characteristics described in this book.

For most of the five groups, the selection was obvious. The following is a description of each of the comparison groups and the highest-ranking team selected for each group.

Comparison Group 1.[1] Assessment results for these six teams are shown in Figure 3.3. This group was part of a university-based study, with doctoral students as part of the research team. The teams were based in a variety of different host organizations. However, projects were carefully selected to ensure that they were comparable in scope and complexity. Projects lasted twelve weeks.

> *Top-Rated Team*—Team 2: Order Cancellation Team. This was the team profiled in Chapter Two. It clearly stood out from the rest. Its speed (5 learning cycles) was much greater than the others (which averaged 1.6 cycles). In fact, one of the teams was evaluated as having no learning cycles. How could that be? Over the course of the entire project, the team never gathered any information or took any actions whatsoever to find out anything members did not know at the beginning. It merely assembled recommendations based on team member perceptions regarding what needed to be done. Regarding depth, the Order Cancellation Team was the only team that successfully reframed its project. Regarding breadth, the team's project had substantial, long-term impact on the organization that greatly exceeded the original project scope.

Comparison Group 2.[2] As shown in Figure 3.4, these four teams were all from the same public utility. They were formed in conjunction with an action learning program for middle managers. Projects lasted from eight to twelve weeks.

> *Top-Rated Team*—Team 8. Cost Reduction Team (see the case description in Chapter Five). The differences among the three teams in this group were not quite as great as they were in the first group, possibly because they were all part of a structured action learning program. Two of the four teams were able to reframe their projects and had an impact on their organizations broader than the scope of their projects. The Cost Reduction Team was selected as the top team in this group because of its greater speed, completing six total cycles during the period. This team also produced results that were clearly superior to the other teams by exceeding ambitious cost reduction targets and developing approaches to cost reduction that are now being used throughout much of the company.

Figure 3.3
Comparison Group 1: Analysis of Speed, Depth, and Breadth

Team	Organization	Speed	Depth		Breadth		Results
		# of Cycles	Project Reframed?	If Yes, Describe.	Impact Outside Project Scope?	If Yes, Describe.	
1. Restructuring	Higher education	1	No		No		Recommendations were not implemented; new team formed in six months.
2. Order Cancellation*	Publishing	5	Yes	From internal operations to strategic marketing issue	Yes	Sparked strategic planning effort and repositioning of company	Team was credited with initiating the competitive repositioning of the company and a sales turnaround.
3. Performance Management	Manufacturing	0	No		No		Team disbanded without making recommendations.
4. Geographic Expansion	Financial services	2	No		No		No known results.
5. Fundraising	Higher education	2	No		No		No known results.
6. Leadership Development	Utility	3	No		No		Recommendations were not accepted.

*Selected as the highest-rated team in the comparison group.

Figure 3.4
Comparison Group 2: Analysis of Speed, Depth, and Breadth

| Team | Organization | Speed | | Depth | | Breadth | | Results |
		# of Cycles	Project Reframed?	If Yes, Describe.	Impact Outside Project Scope?	If Yes, Describe.	Results
7. Staff Empowerment	Utility	2	No		No		No known results.
8. Cost Reduction*	Utility	6	Yes	From materials and process issues to management practice and labor relations issues	Yes		30% cost reduction.
9. Best Practice Dissemination	Utility	3	No		No		100% increase in best practices implemented corporationwide.
10. Reducing Duplicate Operations	Utility	4	Yes	From operations to management practices and workforce involvement issues	Yes		Recommendations made to corporate group; no known results.

*Selected as the highest-rated team in the comparison group.

Comparison Group 3.[3] As shown in Figure 3.5, these four teams were from two different elementary schools that were part of a foundation-funded school improvement initiative. Projects lasted anywhere from a semester to a full school year.

> *Top-Rated Team:* Team 12: Mathematics Improvement Team (see Chapter Six for the full story of this team). The speed of learning in this group was relatively high compared to the other groups. However, only one team—the Mathematics Improvement Team—actually reframed its project. This team provided critical insights that allowed an elementary school in a low socio-economic district to dramatically improve the test scores of its students. Within two years after implementing the team's recommendations, the school moved from the second-lowest to the second-highest-rated school in math scores out of fifteen elementary schools in the district. What did the team learn? They learned that many teachers did not possess the basic knowledge of mathematics needed to be effective math teachers. The team's recommendations also had broad, long-term impact on how the school district purchased classroom materials and provided staff development.

Comparison Group 4.[4] As shown in Figure 3.6, this group consisted of three teams from a mid-sized manufacturing company.

> *Top-Rated Team*—Team 17: Production Scheduling Team (the story of this team appears in Chapter Seven). Two of the three teams in this group were rated fairly high on all three dimensions. However, the Production Scheduling Team was picked as the top because of its greater speed (seven cycles compared to five) and the presence of measurable results. This team began with a narrowly defined issue and ended with recommending the across-the-board restructuring of the company, changes in long-standing policy, and a critical reexamination of corporate culture. When it comes to results, the early signs are very positive: on-time shipments are up and customer complaints are down.

Comparison Group 5. These are the three North American Consolidation teams described earlier in this chapter. Figure 3.7 shows the results of the assessment.[5]

> *Top-Rated Team*—Team 18. North American Consolidation Project—Marketing Team. This was the only team that checked out the underlying assumptions behind the consolidation decision—namely, that a full consolidation would not affect sales and customer service. As a result the consolidation plans were changed substantially. Most of the desired cost savings were achieved, and sales have continued to increase.

Figure 3.5

Comparison Group 3: Analysis of Speed, Depth, and Breadth

Team	Organization	Speed	Depth		Breadth		Results
		# of Cycles	Project Reframed?	If Yes, Describe.	Impact Outside Project Scope?	If Yes, Describe.	
11. Writing Improvement	Public school	6	No		Yes	Approach to staff develop-ment used at other schools.	Student mathematics performance improved 20%.
12. Mathematics Improvement*	Public school	7	Yes	From teach-ing methods to teacher knowledge of subject	Yes	Other schools adopted practices.	Student mathematics performance improved 65%.
13. Reading Improvement	Public school	5	No		No		Reading performance of students continued to decline.
14. Parent Involvement	Public school	3	No		No		Team was disbanded.

*Selected as the highest-rated team in the comparison group.

Figure 3.6
Comparison Group 4: Analysis of Speed, Depth, and Breadth

Team	Organization	Speed		Depth		Breadth		Results
		# of Cycles	Project Reframed?	If Yes, Describe.	Impact Outside Project Scope?	If Yes, Describe.		
15. Inventory Management	Marketing services	4	No		No			Key performance measures showed no improvement. New team was formed one year later.
16. Production Scheduling*	Marketing services	7	Yes	To organization structure, management practices, and culture issues	Yes	Organization has been restructured.		Significant improvements were made in on-time delivery and customer satisfaction.
17. New Product Line	Marketing services	5	Yes	From introducing new product to creating a new division	Yes	New division has been formed and is up and running.		It is too early to assess results.

*Selected as the highest-rated team in the comparison group.

Figure 3.7
Comparison Group 5: Analysis of Speed, Depth, and Breadth

| Team | Organization | Speed | | Depth | | Breadth | | Results |
		# of Cycles	Project Reframed?	If Yes, Describe.	Impact Outside Project Scope?	If Yes, Describe.		
18. North American Consolidation—Marketing*	Manufacturing and distribution	4	No	From consolidating operations to increasing margin contribution	Yes	Attempt to fully consolidate North American operations was abandoned.		Margin contributions from the Canadian market doubled over the next three years. Market share increased as well.
19. North American Consolidation—Customer Service	Manufacturing and distribution	2	No		No			Initial recommendations were not accepted. Team was directed to build plans based on Marketing Team's work.
20. North American Consolidation—Operations	Manufacturing and distribution	2	No		No			Initial recommendations were not accepted. Team was directed to build plans based on Marketing Team's work.

*Selected as the highest-rated team in the comparison group.

Through this assessment of twenty teams, five teams were selected as most representing the characteristics of radical teams. They approached their projects as a learning process (the speed dimension). They reframed their projects (the depth dimension). And they produced results that had widespread impact on their organizations (the breadth dimension). These teams also produced results that were vastly superior to most of the other teams. These are the radical teams we were searching for.

The next chapter will delve deeper into the practices of these five teams and examine what the radical teams did that was different from most other teams in the study. Based on the differences, I will propose a series of concrete action steps that you can take with your own project teams to harness team learning and produce equally powerful results.

chapter
FOUR

Harnessing the Power of Team Learning

The last chapter identified five radical teams, selected because the speed, depth, and breadth of their learning exceeded that of comparable teams; they also appeared to produce superior results. The purpose of this chapter is to describe what radical teams do that allows them to learn more effectively than traditional teams. Another team from each of the five comparison groups will serve as a contrast to the radical team. The second team was usually not the lowest-rated team in each category, but it best represents how the other teams in the comparison group approached their projects. Through this process five pairs were created. As shown in Figure 4.1, each pair included one radical team (one of the teams chosen in the last chapter) and one traditional team.

The next step was to go back and review the information that was available on the five radical teams and the five traditional teams, including learning logs from individual team members, audiotapes of team meetings, and notes of independent observers who sat in on most team meetings. The purpose was to select the concrete actions that most distinguished the radical teams as a group from the traditional teams. These actions were then subdivided into three categories: speed, depth, and breadth. Actions that seemed to influence the speed of the teams were put in

59

Figure 4.1
Teams Selected as Radical and Traditional Teams

Comparison Group	Radical Team	Traditional Team
1	Order Cancellation Team (team 2)	Restructuring Team (team 1)
2	Cost Reduction Team (team 8)	Best Practice Dissemination Team (team 9)
3	Mathematics Improvement Team (team 12)	Reading Improvement Team (team 13)
4	Production Scheduling Team (team 16)	Inventory Management Team (team 15)
5	North American Consolidation—Marketing Team (team 18)	North American Consolidation—Customer Service Team (team 19)

the speed category; those that influenced the depth dimension were put in the depth category, and so on. Figure 4.2 provides a complete list of these practices.

SPEED: RADICAL TEAMS VERSUS TRADITIONAL TEAMS

Consider the following two statements, one from a traditional team and one from a radical team:

> I have prepared a list of five alternative approaches we could take. It seems very straightforward. Research each one—select the best—present our recommendations—and act. We should be able to just compare the options on a spreadsheet, weigh the costs, time, and commitment, and come up with a solution. (From the log of a member of a traditional team)

> As we were gathering information, some of the things that we thought were right were just not so. We were surprised that we were learning new things. We began to challenge ourselves to think of other areas where we might be wrong. We began to look at things we've done for years and years without questioning. We began to look at how other areas of our company were functioning. Was there something that could be learned from them? (From an interview with a member of a radical team)

Figure 4.2
Key Differences Between Radical and Traditional Teams

Radical Teams	Traditional Teams
Speed	
1. Acknowledge uncertainty and the need to learn.	1. Approach projects with certainty and a linear approach to problem solving.
2. Separate facts from assumptions.	2. Tend not to examine assumptions to determine their validity.
3. Act to learn.	3. Act to execute plans.
4. Work to reduce learning cycle time.	4. Are unaware of team learning concepts.
5. Take steps to improve team learning.	5. Are not concerned with team learning.
Depth	
1. Make it safe to take risks.	1. Often create a climate in which it is risky to openly express ideas, admit mistakes, or challenge management.
2. Detect early warning signs.	2. Tend to ignore early warning signs.
3. Explore divergent views.	3. View divergent views and conflicts as roadblocks.
4. Exploit breakdowns to produce breakthroughs.	4. Interpret breakdowns as symptoms of poor team or individual performance.
5. Capture lessons learned from cycle to cycle.	5. Continue working on projects without capturing lessons learned.
6. Reframe projects to reflect deepening understandings.	6. Generally accept without question the way in which their projects have been framed.
Breadth	
1. Uncover connections.	1. Focus on direct routes to solutions.
2. Reach out to influence others.	2. Are often influenced by others.
3. Learn from past projects.	3. Usually start from scratch, often making the same mistakes or reinventing the wheel.
4. Go against the organizational grain.	4. Conform to the prevailing organizational culture.
5. Take responsibility for making things happen elsewhere.	5. Are generally unconcerned about whether their results are applied broadly.

These are two very different comments. The first exudes confidence and control. The second reveals humility and a willingness to learn. These statements reflect the way the two teams handled their projects. For the first team there was little need to find out things the team did not already know, other than exactly how some steps would be implemented and how much things would cost. The second team, after some initial reluctance, felt very comfortable with engaging in a discovery process, recognizing that its own conceptions about the project may be wrong.

By comparing these two teams, as well as the other pairs of teams, it is possible to identify five key differences between radical teams and traditional teams that most affect the speed of team learning. Each difference is described in the sections to follow.

Difference 1: Uncertainty Versus Certainty

Traditional teams generally begin their projects with relative certainty regarding what needs to be done. Team discussions primarily consist of team members asserting their opinions regarding how best to achieve the desired results. Team members seem to be valued by the degree of expertise they possess that is directly related to the problems at hand. In fact, many teams act as if they know what the final answers are going to be, at least generally. All that has to be done is to work out the details. Possessing such certainty, many teams develop comprehensive plans for their entire projects at their first meetings.

In contrast, radical teams openly declare their own ignorance. They recognize that they do not have all the answers. They understand that in order to complete their projects successfully, they will need to discover things that they do not know and that preconceived ideas and solutions are likely to be erroneous and misleading. Team members appreciate the need to engage in a shared learning process in which old perspectives and traditional solutions are abandoned and new approaches discovered. Team members accept the inherent ambiguity of such situations, recognizing that coming up with answers will be neither easy nor quick. They realize that members do not need to possess technical or functional expertise to be useful to the teams. Asking good questions is seen as potentially more valuable than suggesting possible solutions.

Difference 2: Assumptions Versus Facts

In traditional teams, members often present their opinions as indisputable truths without offering any objective evidence to support their validity. In addition, team members often readily accept each other's opinions without questioning. Often such teams seem to be guided by a set of unstated, mutually shared assumptions about their projects. Much of their subsequent work is based on these unsupported assumptions.

In contrast, radical teams seek to make clear and careful distinctions between what they know (facts) and what they believe to be true (assumptions). At early stages, much of their work consists of surfacing assumptions that can be tested to see whether they are true or not. To do so, team members often explicitly present their initial perspectives as assumptions. They challenge each other to verify whether statements are facts or assumptions.

Difference 3: Acting to Learn Versus Executing Plans

Most traditional teams separate the "planning" part of their projects from the "acting" part. Actions are done when it is time to implement detailed, approved plans. The quality of plans is judged, based on the degree to which the project is "on plan." Rarely do most teams ask the following questions:

- What don't we know that we need to know?
- What actions can we take between now and the next meeting to find out what we need to know?
- How can we verify that what we are assuming is actually true?

Team meetings generally end with no agreement to act other than to meet again within a few weeks.

In contrast, with radical teams almost every meeting represents the end of one learning cycle and the beginning of another. In fact, teams find clever ways to complete learning cycles between meetings, such as telephone conferences and electronic exchanges via computer and others. Team members often challenge each other to speed up learning cycles by posing such questions as

- What might we find out by the next time we meet that would tell us whether "X" is true or not?
- Why do we need to wait until our next meeting? Let's share what we have on e-mail as soon as we know something?

The teams look for opportunities to try quick experiments or check out hunches.

Difference 4: Reducing Learning Cycle Time
Versus Reducing Project Cycle Time

First, let us make a clear distinction between project cycle time and learning cycle time. *Project cycle time* refers to the total time needed to complete a project from beginning to end. Many organizations have goals to reduce the project cycle time from project to project. This is especially true when it comes to trying to get products to market faster. Traditional teams are primarily concerned with project cycle time, that is, with completing their projects on or before schedule. They develop project plans that promise to get them to the finish line as directly as possible. They periodically stop to see if they are on plan. They focus on completing stages and getting through "stage-gates" on or before schedule. They try to anticipate potential roadblocks early. Discussions are task-focused, avoiding digressions or diversions that are not directly related to that project.

In contrast, *learning cycle time* has to do with how long it takes for teams to complete learning cycles. Radical teams are aware of their learning cycle time and take purposeful steps to reduce cycle time as a means of accelerating the learning process. They are still committed to completing projects on time. However, their aim is not to get to the finish line as quickly and directly as possible, because there is a good chance that the finish line will move as a result of what they have learned. Instead, the goal is to learn as quickly as possible—to discover in a few weeks what might otherwise take months and years of painful trial-and-error learning. The key is to engage in rapid-fire learning cycles. Therefore, radical teams continuously explore ways to decrease learning cycle time, challenging themselves with questions such as

- How can we quickly test out these assumptions?
- Can we take advantage of an upcoming event to try out some ideas?
- Can we accelerate our meeting schedules by using advanced technology (groupware, video-teleconferencing, telephone conferencing) to substitute for face-to-face communications?

Difference 5. Improving Team Learning
Versus Improving Team Dynamics

Both traditional teams and radical teams occasionally stop and discuss how well they are doing as teams. But they seem to pay attention to different things. Traditional teams tend to emphasize running efficient meetings and communicating effectively with each other. They tend to focus these reviews on questions such as, Do we stay on task? Do we listen to what others are saying? Do we avoid dominating the discussion? and Are we respectful of each other when there are disagreements?

In contrast, radical teams seem more concerned with how well they are learning as a team. They periodically stop and ask questions such as, How well are we separating facts from assumptions? To what degree are we taking actions that will allow us to learn quickly? How can we speed up our learning cycles? and Do we tend to emphasize certain parts of the learning cycle (such as planning or acting) over other steps (such as reflecting)? By periodically reviewing how well they are learning, radical teams can identify areas to focus on to improve their learning over the course of their projects.

DEPTH: RADICAL TEAMS VERSUS OTHER TEAMS

Here is another pair of statements, one from a traditional team member and one from a radical team member:

> This was a frustrating meeting. One person felt that we should try to find out why we were having problems implementing best practices to begin with and not just come up with a better way to communicate them. We listened politely for awhile, but he just wouldn't let go of it. The rest of us felt that we were on the right track and that we knew what we were doing. That wasn't our job. We pulled out our project definition. It stated clearly that we were to enhance communication and education. (From an interview with a team member of a traditional team)

> At first we just treated the symptoms. It was like taking a decongestant or cough syrup when you have a cold. Then we started to get at the underlying cause. That was like taking an antibiotic. (From an interview with a team member of a radical team)

These statements provide important insights into the depth dimension. Early on in their projects both teams had detected signs that they were just scratching the surface. The first team quickly dismissed such an idea without seriously considering the possibility that it might be heading down the wrong track. The second team became intrigued by the idea that it could produce more profound and lasting solutions if it considered the need to reframe its project. In the following sections I discuss the key differences between radical teams and traditional teams that seem to allow radical teams to transform their basic understanding of the nature of their projects, whereas traditional teams do not.

Difference 1: Safety Versus Risk

The most critical difference that affects the depth of learning may be whether members feel that it is safe to express opinions openly, admit mistakes and errors, acknowledge that they do not have the answers, ask for help, question original goals, and challenge management direction. Radical teams purposefully work over the course of projects to establish team norms that promote openness and risk taking. They intentionally test the water to see how safe it is to take risks. They gradually escalate risk-taking behaviors over the course of projects. And they try to make others in the organization feel safe to take risks related to their projects.

Difference 2: Detecting Early Warning Signs Versus Ignoring Them

Think about a project team meeting you have attended when, for the first time, there was some objective evidence that the team might be headed in the wrong direction. What did the team do? Most teams tend to ignore any information that contradicts the framing assumptions about the project. For various reasons teams often do not take the new information seriously, and the framing assumptions persist in the face of evidence that they are faulty. Here is how one team member recorded his perceptions of such an exchange in his personal log: "It was so clear to me. All of the information we gathered told me our approach was wrong. I just couldn't convince anybody else what it meant."

In contrast, radical teams relentlessly search for the ground truth. They seek out information that can be objectively confirmed or disconfirmed to the satisfaction of team members. Over the course of their projects, as more and more information is made available, they carefully separate verifiable evidence from unsupported perceptions. They follow the facts wherever they might lead. As teams, they collectively build shared understandings by carefully and systematically interpreting and drawing conclusions from the information that they have gathered.

Difference 3: Exploring Divergent Views Versus Dismissing Them

Think about a time when you were in a project team meeting and there was a difference of opinion between two team members. How was the situation handled? What were the results? In most teams such conversations resemble a tennis match. Every volley is greeted by a quick response, the "tennis ball" being hit back over the court as quickly and forcefully as possible. In some cases this conversation is polite and respectful; in others, aggressive and quarrelsome. In either case such conversations produce winners and losers. One side prevails, convincing the group as a whole that his or her perspective is the right one. The other side's viewpoint is dismissed.

In radical teams such conversations are approached much differently. It is not just that people try to understand each other's perspectives before presenting their own. It's that members put aside any preconceptions and are genuinely open to being influenced by other points of view. They willingly explore other views, seeking to understand what led others to the conclusions they have reached. Team members are careful to present any objective information they have and then invite other team members to confirm or disconfirm the conclusions they have drawn. The aim is to create a shared understanding among team members, not to have a debate.

Difference 4: Breakthroughs Versus Breakdowns

Frustration, interpersonal conflict, lack of progress—most teams see these as signs that they are in trouble. The expectation seems to be that projects should be completed with minimal frustration, conflict, disruption, or detours.

In contrast, radical teams expect such breakdowns to occur and try to use them to produce project breakthroughs. They recognize that the tension underlying these symptoms may provoke new insights. In fact, in the twenty teams that we studied, almost every time a team reframed a project, the reframing was preceded by a breakdown of some sort: a heated disagreement among team members, a long period of time when no progress was being made, noticeable signs of frustration. Rather than avoid impasses and uncomfortable situations, radical teams often stop and reflect on "what is happening here now." Such reflections often highlight the major roadblocks and blind spots that are prohibiting the team from looking at its problem in a different way. And such reflections, however uncomfortable, are understood to be natural and necessary for the team to dismiss old assumptions about the project and develop fundamentally new understandings.

Difference 5: Capturing Lessons Learned Versus Moving to the Next Cycle

Most project teams do not stop and attempt to capture what has been learned at the end of one cycle before moving on to the next. Seldom do most teams ask themselves, "So what do we know now that we did not know before?" or "How does this new information change how we are looking at our project?" or "To what degree do our original assumptions still make sense?"

In contrast, radical teams collectively and explicitly capture what they have learned at the end of each cycle. Lessons learned are treated as tangible team products, just as important as the other deliverables produced. In some ways the lessons learned are seen as more important because they often have the potential of producing a broad and pervasive impact on their organizations, much beyond the original boundaries of the projects.

Difference 6: Reframing Projects Versus Containing Projects

Most teams do not change the way their projects are originally defined, even if there is concrete evidence that much bigger issues are involved. Why? It might be politically risky because reframing often means challenging the conventional wisdom or prevailing organizational culture. In addition, teams might be concerned that they will be perceived as overstepping their boundaries, and their motives for doing so might be questioned. Moreover, it will likely take more time and effort on everyone's part if the project is reframed. As a result teams are reluctant to reframe their projects, even when the team knows it is the right thing to do.

In contrast, radical teams recognize that reframing is likely the only way to produce desired project outcomes. They are not afraid to recognize that the way their projects are defined may be the real problem. Radical teams also take whatever steps are needed to renegotiate their projects with sponsors and champions so as to reflect the reframed understandings of their projects. When reframing, they consider everything up for grabs, including the project goals, end deliverables, resources requirements, team membership, and time lines.

BREADTH: RADICAL TEAMS VERSUS OTHER TEAMS

The following statements reveal two fundamentally different attitudes regarding projects:

> We can't solve all of the company's problems. We have a clearly defined project. Let's finish our work and get on with things. We can only do so much, and that's not our job anyway. (From the log of a team member of a traditional team)

> There's a host of other issues involved—marketing, financial, and operational. And they're all linked together. I think we need to stop before we go any further and make sure they [top management] are really serious about things and whether they think we're overstepping our bounds if we deal with some of the bigger issues. (Comments made by a team member of a radical team, as reported by an observer)

Whereas traditional teams are content to keep their projects restricted within predetermined boundaries, radical teams refuse to let any predetermined definitions of project scope influence their projects. Radical teams let their projects explode. Based on what is learned, narrowly defined issues come to be seen as "systems" problems. Simple, single-faceted problems now become complex, multifaceted issues. It does not deter such teams that their projects are becoming bigger, require more work, and touch on controversial issues. The teams seem more concerned with doing what is right for their organizations than what is expedient and safe.

When it comes to the breadth of team learning, there are five key differences between radical teams and traditional teams regarding how they approach their projects.

Difference 1: Uncovering Connections Versus Tunnel Vision

Too many teams have tunnel vision. They start their projects by defining them as specifically and narrowly as possible. They then limit themselves to investigating a fairly narrow band of forces and factors, such as designated functional areas (marketing, production, research and development, and so on) or specific business units (certain geographical areas, certain product lines, certain departments).

Between the beginning and end of projects the scope does not change. If they stumble on information that factors outside their project scope may be involved, they seem to be overwhelmed by the complexity and usually decide to retain a narrow focus.

In contrast, radical teams seek to uncover connections among a range of forces and factors that might seem initially unrelated. For example, they might begin to see how internal company issues are related to external business conditions such as changing customer needs, new competition, shifting technologies, and other marketplace trends. They begin to understand how the various functional specializations such as marketing, production, research and development, and finance are all interconnected. They come to recognize that issues previously considered the province of a specific business unit or geographical area are, in fact, organizationwide issues. Radical teams are skilled at simplifying the complex interrelationships among a wide range of factors in a way that they can be understood by the team and clearly communicated to others. They understand that cause-effect relationships often have a time lag. They appreciate that multiple symptoms often derive from a single root cause. They recognize that organizational actions designed to solve one problem often unintentionally cause many others.

Difference 2: Influencing Others Versus Being Influenced

For every project there are usually many different stakeholders: people who will need to support decisions, people who will implement final recommendations, and people who will be affected by what happens in the project. Most teams are relatively passive in the stance they take toward these individuals. In many cases they do not even discuss who the key stakeholders are. And if teams do identify them, it is frequently presumed that they will automatically provide whatever support will be needed later on. However, the reality is that others in the organization often attempt to influence teams by second-guessing what they have done, questioning recommendations, and undermining implementation. This phenomenon is most evident when teams begin to reframe their projects, moving into issues or areas seemingly outside their jurisdiction.

Radical teams take a different approach. From the beginning of their projects, they seek to proactively influence people who might possess control, power, or authority over their projects. They explicitly identify a range of stakeholders and reach out to them. But the teams are also smart. They recognize that others in the organization might push for more conventional approaches; as a result, they do not blindly accept input provided by others. At times they decide to "fly under the radar," taking quick actions in ways that will result in the least visibility and generate the least resistance from their organizations. They carefully control communications related to their projects, determining what will be communicated, when, how, and to whom. Their aim is to manage whole organizations so that the projects can have maximum impact. Aware that their projects might take them in directions and into areas not initially anticipated, the teams work closely with champions and sponsors to make sure that project redefinition and expansion is supported. The teams understand that for sponsors and champions to accept project reframing, the sponsors and champions themselves will need to undergo a surrogate learning process in which their own assumptions are tested. As a result the teams work closely with champions and sponsors to prepare them for the possibility of project reframing. In many cases sponsors and champions, because of their knowledge of and power in organizations, serve as indispensable allies to teams in managing the rest of the organizations when reframing occurs.

Difference 3: Learning from Past Projects Versus Starting from Scratch

Most organizations have lengthy project histories from which to learn. Examples include computer conversions that brought the company to its knees and alienated many customers, new-product launches that were delayed past the point where marketplace advantage was lost, and so on. Yet rarely do teams examine past projects from which they might gain important insights to inform the projects at hand. Most teams seem insistent on making the same mistakes again or, when an approach has worked, reinventing the wheel. Sometimes teams are unaware of relevant aspects of their companies' histories. Other times they know about past projects but seem to avoid learning from them. Why this failure to learn from the past? There are probably several reasons. Learning about the past often requires additional work. Also it is human nature to be somewhat arrogant, thinking that the situations we are facing have never been encountered before and to be reluctant to learn from those who have tried similar things in the past.

In contrast, radical teams purposefully examine their organizations' past histories, seeking to derive information and insights that can be applied to the current projects. In most cases radical teams have members or have access to individuals who possess long-term organizational perspectives. However, radical teams do not look at the past in ways that result in the perpetuation of conventional or traditional project solutions. On the contrary, they are primarily concerned that past failures not be repeated. They recognize that they will likely fall into the same traps that others have fallen into if they are not aware of the traps. At the same time they do not dismiss the past as a series of failed projects and poor judgments. Radical teams also study project successes, recognizing that there is likely to be considerable wisdom that can be derived by looking at what worked in the past.

Difference 4: Going Against the Organizational Grain Versus Reflecting the Organization's Culture

The previous description of radical teams contains several apparent paradoxes, such as reaching out to influence others and yet keeping a healthy distance and learning from the past while trying to come up with novel solutions. Rather than paradoxes, I prefer to think of these as creative tensions. Maybe the greatest tension relates to corporate culture.

Culture is simply "the way we do things around here." At its best, culture represents the accumulated wisdom regarding what has made firms successful over the years. However, given changing business realities, aspects of the culture may be harmful rather than helpful. Conservative, risk-aversive companies may need to become more aggressive. Internally focused companies may need to become more market-driven. Entrepreneurial companies may need to become more formal and bureaucratic. As might be expected, the majority of project teams seem to accept the prevailing company culture without question. In fact, they tend to be unaware that an organizational culture exists and is influencing how the teams approach their projects.

In contrast, radical teams deliberately separate themselves from aspects of the culture that might impede learning and reframing. They identify elements of the culture that could hurt their projects. Then in these areas the teams try to establish their own miniculture that goes against the grain. They establish explicit team norms that violate aspects of the culture. For example, a project team existing in a hierarchical, risk-aversive culture established the following ground rule: *Don't ask for permission. Just do it.*

Radical teams also engage in symbolic actions that are designed to be counter-cultural. For example, a project team made up entirely of managers invited several bargaining unit leaders to join their team as full and equal members. Any time the team made its presentation to senior management, the bargaining unit members took the lead. Such actions were designed to confront the patronizing us-versus-them culture the team felt continued to persist in the organization.

Difference 5: Taking Responsibility for Making Things Happen Versus Letting Things Happen

At the end of their projects, most teams are shy and reluctant to suggest that their work has the potential for widespread impact in their organizations. They present their final deliverables and, washing their hands of the projects, let others determine whether there is the potential for a wider impact. The teams do not personally or actively take steps to try to make things happen elsewhere in their firms. Even teams that successfully reframe their projects often keep what they have learned to themselves.

Radical teams distinguish themselves from other teams by deliberately sharing what they have accomplished and transferring what they have learned to others. The motive is not self-promotion but to expand the impact of the projects and achieve more powerful results. Radical teams do more than just present their deliverables and insights with the larger organizations. They seek to make things happen elsewhere. They are not afraid to push their organizations to take actions they might not have taken otherwise. In some cases the teams or team members assume formal responsibilities for making things happen throughout the organization. At other times teams turn over responsibilities to other teams or individuals. In either case the project teams do whatever is possible to maximize the impact of their projects on their organizations.

ACTION STEPS OVERVIEW

This chapter has described the major differences between radical teams and other teams. The end product of these comparisons is a series of action steps for each dimension: speed, depth, and breadth. As shown in Figure 4.3, these action steps constitute a practical series of guidelines that can be used by other project teams to improve their learning approaches.

```
┌─────────────────────────────────────────────────────────────────────┐
│                          Figure 4.3                                   │
│                  Action Steps for Radical Teams                       │
│  ───────────────────────────────────────────────────────────────     │
│                                                                       │
│  Speed                                                                │
│  Action Step 1: Acknowledge uncertainty and the need to learn.        │
│  Action Step 2: Separate facts from assumptions.                      │
│  Action Step 3: Act to learn.                                         │
│  Action Step 4: Reduce learning cycle time.                           │
│  Action Step 5: Improve team learning.                                │
│                                                                       │
│  Depth                                                                │
│  Action Step 1: Make it safe.                                         │
│  Action Step 2: Detect early warning signs.                           │
│  Action Step 3: Explore divergent views.                              │
│  Action Step 4: Exploit breakdowns to produce breakthroughs.          │
│  Action Step 5: Capture lessons learned from cycle to cycle.          │
│  Action Step 6: Reframe projects to reflect deepening understandings. │
│                                                                       │
│  Breadth                                                              │
│  Action Step 1: Uncover connections.                                  │
│  Action Step 2: Reach out to influence others.                        │
│  Action Step 3: Learn from the past.                                  │
│  Action Step 4: Go against the organizational grain.                  │
│  Action Step 5: Make things happen elsewhere.                         │
│                                                                       │
└─────────────────────────────────────────────────────────────────────┘
```

These action steps serve as the core of the rest of this book. In Part Two—beginning with the next chapter—each of the action steps is presented in detail. Speed, depth, and breadth will each be discussed in separate chapters, along with application exercises that will allow you to apply these action steps with your own team.

Radical Teams in Action

chapter
FIVE

High-Speed Learning
Action Steps to Increase the Speed of Team Learning

> *There have been a lot of iterations. It's like reducing a sauce by half.*
> *It's a more flavorful sauce, a more complex group of ingredients,*
> *but the end result is simpler. We made it easier to use . . .*
> *by continually challenging ourselves to find what is essential.*
>
> From an interview with a team member[1]

Radical teams approach projects as a process of high-speed learning. From the outset they recognize that they do not possess all of the answers and that they need to produce new knowledge and understandings as quickly as possible. They are consumed by the need to reduce learning cycle time, figure things out in weeks that might otherwise take months or years. This chapter presents the following action steps to help teams increase the speed of their learning:

Action Step 1: Acknowledge uncertainty and the need to learn.

Action Step 2: Separate facts from assumptions.

77

Action Step 3: Act to learn.

Action Step 4: Reduce learning cycle time.

Action Step 5: Improve team learning.

Application exercises are provided throughout the chapter. In some cases alternative exercises are offered that serve the same or a similar purpose. A team need not use all of these exercises; each team should simply select the exercises that best meet its needs.

The following story illustrates how one of the radical teams successfully enhanced its speed of learning and managed its project as a discovery process.

Cost Reduction Team

Public utilities are in the process of deregulating, and the survival of Community Electric (a pseudonym) is at stake. Other competitors with less than half the fixed costs are poised to compete directly with the company. Dramatic and immediate cost reduction is essential for Community Electric's survival. Over the years many attempts have been made to reduce costs. However, the cost gap between Community Electric and its potential competitors remains unchanged. Several factors are contributing to Community Electric's high costs: the company has a fairly senior workforce (most have over twenty years tenure); it operates in a strongly unionized environment; and local environmental regulations restrict it to using raw materials, with much higher costs than those used by potential competitors.

Recently, the company launched an ambitious action learning program designed with a dual purpose in mind: (1) to help middle managers develop the skills they need to transition to a deregulated environment and (2) to find solutions to some of the company's toughest problems. Several learning teams were formed, and each was assigned a project. Not surprisingly, many of the projects had to do with getting costs out of the business.

One such team was charged with reducing repair costs by 20 percent annually. When the project team was formed, the division manager advised the team that this project had been specifically chosen for the action learning program because it represented a complex, difficult challenge and that there were no easy answers. He told the team that he personally did not know how to solve this problem. He also said that he suspected that both he and the team would need to be open to changing their old ways of doing things if the company was going to be successful competing in the new world of deregulation. He also said that he would lend his personal support to the team throughout the process.

Cycle 1: At its first session the team began exploring the project. A few team members were convinced that there were more significant ways to reduce costs but that top management would not implement them because of union pressure. An example given was the increased use of modified voltage transformers (MVTs). In the words of one member: "We can save all the money on MVTs, and [the vice president] won't do it because he's afraid of the union. It will make it look like he doesn't care about safety. But there's nothing unsafe about MVTs." Other than by using MVTs, the team seemed stumped as to how they were going to reduce costs by 20 percent. "This is a stupid exercise," one member commented. "If there was a way to get costs out of things, don't you think we would have already done it?"

As part of the action learning process, the team was guided to come up with a list of assumptions about the project that needed to be checked out to see whether they were true or not. After some discussion the team identified two key assumptions: (1) that the increased use of MVTs had the potential for significant cost reductions and (2) that there were limited opportunities to save costs other than the increased use of MVTs. The team was then asked to identify some quick steps it could take that would verify to the satisfaction of the entire team that these assumptions were either true or not true. The team came up with the following steps:

- Gather information on all the areas where MVTs were currently being used and not being used.

- Talk to key managers to discuss the potential use of MVTs in other places.

- Hold brainstorming meetings to see if there were other ways to reduce repair costs that the team had not discovered.

The team agreed to meet again in two weeks.

The next meeting began with a review of the information that had been gathered. Team members were surprised with what they found out:

- The company was already using MVTs in just about every application where it made sense, and neither the vice president nor the union had any problem with using it as long as basic safety precautions were followed.

- There were many possible ways to reduce costs other than those identified by the team, including changing construction standards, improving contractor performance, and altering basic engineering methods. As one member put it, "We realize it's a lot bigger than we thought it was."

Cycle 2: The next steps focused on broadening the fact-finding process to include a wider range of potential cost reduction ideas. After about a month and a few interim meetings to check progress, the team met to review the various cost reduction ideas. When combined, these suggestions produced only a 10 percent reduction in repair costs. The only way to reduce costs further was to lay off bargaining unit staff, and the team was convinced that this was not going to happen. Here is how one team member described the dilemma: "It became clear that the only way to save 20 percent was to cut staff, and we knew that we couldn't recommend this."

Cycle 3: The team presented an update to the sponsor, reporting that only a 10 percent reduction in costs looked achievable. The sponsor responded that 10 percent was not good enough. He reinforced his earlier statement that there were no sacred cows. In fact, he fully expected that one source of cost reductions would derive from labor savings and that, if the union wanted to keep the company viable, it would have to support staff reductions.

Cycle 4: The team went back to the drawing board. The team met with union representatives to explore how to reduce labor costs. The union was more receptive to the proposals than had been anticipated, as long as the union contract was followed to the letter. In practical terms this meant that staff reductions would need to be phased in over several years.

Cycle 5: The team was now confident that it could produce another 10 percent in cost reductions, for a 20 percent total, through additional labor savings. The team shared the good news with its sponsor, who, somewhat surprisingly, challenged them to go further. He was convinced that there were opportunities for cost savings that the team was still missing. He said that the only way the company was going to survive was to find a different way of thinking and working.

The team went back and reviewed the cost reduction ideas that had been explored since the beginning of the project, looking for any possibilities for further reductions. Several ideas had been dismissed at the very beginning as unpractical; some would require that managers make fundamental changes in how they manage the business on a daily basis. For example, there was a long-standing practice of doing emergency jobs twice. One crew would go out immediately and fix the problem temporarily. Another crew would go out later and fix it permanently. Significant cost savings could be achieved by fixing the problem only once. However, several team members were convinced that double checking was absolutely necessary to make sure the job was completed correctly.

The team had a heated discussion about this idea and about other suggestions that had been rejected early in the project. Several team members argued strongly for them and others against them. After a few hours the team seemed at a stalemate, firmly entrenched in two camps. One of the opponents to the proposed ideas said that he could not see himself standing in front of the vice president of operations and making these recommendations. He would look stupid. It would appear as if he had not been doing his job over the years. Senior managers would be thinking, "If these are such good ideas, why weren't they doing this already? Why are they finding this out now?" Things got easier from this point on. The team realized that the fear of looking stupid was not a good reason for failing to propose a final set of cost reduction steps that affected the way they managed their business on a daily basis. The team decided to recommend these additional cost savings.

Cycle 6: The team now felt that it had created the basic framework for a comprehensive cost reduction plan that would reduce repair costs by 30 percent. All it would take was to work out the specifics and develop a detailed implementation plan. The recommendations were proposed and adopted a few weeks later.

The story of the Cost Reduction Team illustrates the power of high-speed learning. The team completed more learning cycles during the same period of time than did the other teams that started and ended their projects at the same time (see Figure 5.1).

At least three major breakthroughs occurred as a result of this process. The first was the discovery that a 10 percent reduction could be achieved through a broad range of ideas the team had not considered previously and not through the increased use of MVTs. The second was that another 10 percent could be accomplished through union-supported labor reductions phased in over several years. The third breakthrough was that a final 10 percent could be accomplished if team

Figure 5.1
Team Learning Map: Cost Reduction Team

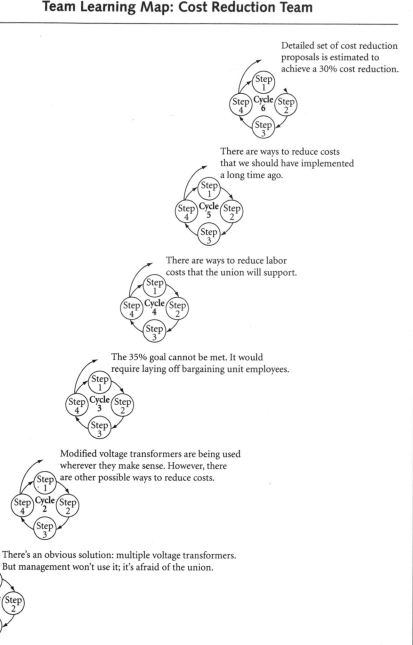

Detailed set of cost reduction proposals is estimated to achieve a 30% cost reduction.

There are ways to reduce costs that we should have implemented a long time ago.

There are ways to reduce labor costs that the union will support.

The 35% goal cannot be met. It would require laying off bargaining unit employees.

Modified voltage transformers are being used wherever they make sense. However, there are other possible ways to reduce costs.

There's an obvious solution: multiple voltage transformers. But management won't use it; it's afraid of the union.

members acknowledged that some of their own routine management practices were obsolete and inefficient and that they were willing to change.

What led to these breakthroughs was the speed of learning. By engaging in rapid learning cycles, the team kept expanding its understandings of the problem through real action in the real world. But what exactly did the Cost Reduction Team and the other radical teams *do* that allowed them to learn faster? In the sections to follow I describe five key actions that radical teams engage in that seem to most accelerate the speed of their learning.

ACTION STEP 1: ACKNOWLEDGE UNCERTAINTY AND THE NEED TO LEARN

Over two thousand years ago, Socrates told his followers that real learning can occur only after one acknowledges one's ignorance. When business realities are shifting constantly, each of us is increasingly faced with new situations or challenged to produce results we do not know how to produce. Radical teams begin their projects with the recognition that the world is throwing problems at them that they do not know how to handle—at least at the present time. Under these conditions what professionals need most is not a reservoir of answers but the ability to find answers. Thus, when sitting down at a conference table with a team for the first time, the best response is to operate from a premise of "I don't know" as opposed to "I know."

Teams need to stand back and look at their projects in terms of the big picture. They are probably facing tasks or problems that have emerged from underlying discontinuities in business conditions. Simply stated, the game has changed—whether it be due to changing markets, technologies, competition, customers, political and governmental factors or, most likely, some combination of these. In the case of the Cost Reduction Team, the discontinuities are clear: deregulation accompanied by fiercely aggressive competitors who enjoy the advantages of lower costs. The things that have made the company successful—its conservative, hierarchical management structure, its way of dealing with bargaining unit employees, and its highly bureaucratic daily procedures—may no longer make sense. In fact, team members needed to recognize that, at some basic level, they themselves were part of the problem, as embodied in their own unquestioned practices. The team's sponsor tried to convey that notion when, at the very beginning of the project, he challenged the team to come up with a different way of thinking and doing work.

As a first step teams need to openly and explicitly acknowledge that they are tackling projects with high levels of uncertainty and that viable solutions will need to be discovered as part of a learning process. They need to admit that they lack all the knowledge needed to solve the problems. They need to admit that their own ways of looking at projects may be deceiving, based on assumptions that are not supported by objective evidence. Remember, several indicators might alert teams that they are tackling projects such as these:

- One or more unsuccessful attempts have been made to solve these problems in the past.

- These are new or unknown situations the companies have not faced before.

- Dramatic results and extensive improvements in performance are being called for.

- The problems are linked to a broad range of other organizational issues and factors.

Not all of these indicators need to be present. In fact, at the beginning of projects it is likely that the signs of uncertainty will be faint and limited. However, over the course of projects such symptoms usually become more evident as teams develop deeper understandings of their projects. After projects are complete, many teams look back and comment how obvious it should have been that they were tackling projects with high levels of uncertainty.

Take the Cost Reduction Team as an example. Several of these characteristics were present at the beginning of the project, most notably that huge leaps in performance were being sought (20 percent reduction in overhead costs) and that the project had been tackled unsuccessfully several times in the past (previous cost reduction initiatives had produced only incremental improvements). As the project progressed, other indicators became apparent: that there were no easy answers (like the use of MVTs) and that the problem was interconnected with a broad range of other organizational issues.

As a member of a project team there are several things you can do to help your team acknowledge the uncertainty that exists with projects. First, at the beginning of each project, take a close look at the project and determine whether, in your opinion, any of the indicators listed appear to be present. If so, invite your fellow team members to share their perceptions of the nature of the project and to discuss any implications regarding how the team needs to approach it. For example, let us say that several other project teams have unsuccessfully tried to solve the same problem in the past. The obvious implication is that your team will need to adopt a fundamentally different approach. Or let us say that the project represents a new situation for the organization. The team cannot assume that what worked in other circumstances will necessarily work here.

The following exercise will help you assess the degree of uncertainty that exists with projects and whether the radical teamwork approach described in this book is needed.

APPLICATION EXERCISE 5.1: RADICAL PROJECT CHECKLIST

The following is an exercise you can use with teams to look for signs of uncertainty.

1. For each item on the checklist to follow, place an "X" in the appropriate column ("Yes" or "No") to signify whether, in your opinion, this characteristic applies to the project.

2. For each item rated Yes, describe the implications for the project, that is, how the project team will need to approach the project differently than it might otherwise if this characteristic were not present.

3. Discuss your answers with each other and explore.

Characteristics of the Project	Yes	No	If Yes, what are the implications?
One or more unsuccessful attempts have been made to solve this problem in the past.			
This is a new or unknown situation the company has not faced before.			
Dramatic results and extensive improvements are needed.			
This problem is linked to a broad range of other organizational issues and factors.			

Avoid Preconceived Solutions

Similarly, it is essential that project teams recognize that preconceived solutions are not likely to produce the desired results and that projects need to be approached as blank slates. This is often hard to do for several reasons. There are strong pressures and incentives for teams to jump immediately to the finish line, propose solutions, and start taking action. It is human nature to do so. The proposed solutions may be derived from deeply held personal or professional beliefs. Most team members, with the best of intentions, want to produce positive outcomes quickly and therefore would love to get on with things, decide what is going to be done, and start taking action. It may not be possible to quickly gather information that will unambiguously demonstrate that the solutions are inadequate. Also, given the increasing demands on people's time in most organizations, there is little tolerance for meetings and projects that take longer than they have to.

However, in spite of these pressures, before a team delves into its work its members need to allow for the possibility that preconceived solutions may not work. One simple technique for overcoming this barrier is called Checking Your Baggage.[2] At their very first meeting team members take a few minutes and write down their perspectives about the topic they are working on and what they think the team's recommendations should be if the recommendations were being made today. One by one, team members describe their initial perspectives about the team's problem. As each person shares his or her viewpoint, other team members listen carefully and ask for clarifications as needed. The purpose is to understand, not to debate or defend specific ideas. After everyone has expressed a viewpoint, the team agrees to temporarily "check our baggage"—to leave these opinions and ideas at the door and proceed to take an objective, zero-based look at the issue at hand. The exercise provides an opportunity for team members to express their initial hunches and beliefs about possible solutions and recommendations. Doing so allows all members to feel that their ideas have been heard.

After everyone has expressed their ideas regarding possible solutions, team members agree to check their baggage and begin a journey of discovery together. They agree that the perspectives they brought to the session will be shelved temporarily and that the team will explore the topic and reach conclusions together. Doing so helps teams recognize that coming up with true solutions—solutions that will have long-term impact and that everyone fully supports—will take patience, objectivity, and teamwork. (Although it was first used with teachers, the Checking Your Baggage exercise has since been used with many different project teams in many different organizations.)

Pose Questions

It is extremely useful for teams to get in the habit of posing questions rather than offering solutions. This can be done in several ways. First, as a whole team state your team's project in terms of a question to be answered rather than a task to be completed. For example, the Cost Reduction Team stated its problem as follows: *How do we reduce repair costs by 20 percent?* This is a simple technique but it does, from the outset, subtly communicate the team's intention to engage in an inquiry and discovery process rather than traditional problem solving.

A second method is to periodically set aside a block of time for asking questions. During this period no declarative statements are allowed, only questions. Such an exercise can be initiated by asking the following starter question: *What questions do we need to be able to answer to achieve breakthrough results on this project that we can't answer now?*

A third method is color questioning, which takes the idea even further (Pacanowsky, 1995).[3] Questions are divided into three color categories: red for facts; green for creative, imaginative ideas; and blue for opinions and value judgments. Teams develop questions as a group, focusing on one color category at a time. Usually these questions are recorded in three columns on a flip chart, with each column in the corresponding color.

ACTION STEP 2: SEPARATE ASSUMPTIONS FROM FACTS

I was recently introduced to the vice president of research and development of a pharmaceutical corporation. It was a short, casual conversation, less than five minutes long, in which I tried to encapsulate the radical team approach. "At its most basic level," I said, "the work of project teams is to surface and check out assumptions." He responded, "What you are telling me is nothing new. You need to verify the assumptions you are making. That's just common sense."

Afterward I realized that I had failed to adequately explain the inscrutability of assumptions. Assumptions are not merely unsubstantiated facts. You cannot generate a list of them and then tick them off one by one and decide whether they are true or not. Assumptions are not "out there"; they are "in here." They are in our minds, reflecting our internal pictures of the world. They represent what Peter Senge calls our *mental models* (1994) and Thomas Kuhn labels *paradigms* (1970). These internal pictures are often hidden and unrecognized. We are frequently not aware that they exist.

Take a look at the set of assumptions held by members of the Cost Reduction Team. The most obvious was that all of the savings could be realized through the increased use of MVTs. There were many other assumptions that the team was not even aware it was making. Together their assumptions reflected a complex and integrated internal picture of the world, a world in which

- Senior executives are cowardly and timid, afraid to do what is best for the organization and afraid to take on a powerful union.
- The workforce is pampered, unmotivated, and unaccountable.
- Middle managers such as themselves have done everything they can over the years to run a cost-effective and efficient operation, and yet, as one member put it, "we get it from both sides."

For them, this project constituted a meaningless and insulting exercise. For them, these were not assumptions at all. They were indisputable facts. Team members often pointed to concrete evidence to support their internal pictures of the world. For instance, during a coffee break one member passionately told the story of a fellow manager whom the company did not back up in a dispute with the union. The manager had written up an employee who was clearly not doing his job, and the employee filed a grievance. During the grievance hearing the manager was personally vilified by the union, and his superiors never did anything to support him. The grievance was settled in the employee's favor. After the story was finished, I asked when this incident occurred. The storyteller responded, "Oh, I think it was '73 or '74."

Team composition has a lot to do with the strength of assumptions. The more team members are alike—sharing similar backgrounds, experiences, and responsibilities—the more likely they are to embrace the same internal picture of the world. Members of the Cost Reduction Team—all middle managers having long tenure with the company—held a remarkably similar internal picture that resulted in a common series of assumptions about the project. It is also likely that top management had its own internal picture and that frontline employees had theirs as well. It is likely that, during coffee breaks, individuals in these groups told similar stories that showed their pictures to be the true ones. This web of internal pictures is what maintains the status quo.

To deal with the business realities that exist today (not 1973 or 1974), radical teams need to strip away these layers of assumptions and reveal what Pascale and Miller (1999) have labeled the "ground truth"—the current business realities that exist when examined without pre- or misconception (p. 67). To do so, as much as possible teams need to clearly see the assumptions *as assumptions*—not facts—and treat them as such. Teams must recognize the difference between an assumption and a fact. An *assumption* is a premise that is not supported by objective evidence or concrete information. A *fact* is a premise that is supported by objective evidence or concrete information.

How can teams do this? At the beginning of projects, teams need to do their best to separate assumptions from facts. Although seemingly a straightforward process, in reality it is very subtle. Even in teams that are fairly homogeneous, team members are often surprised to learn that what they consider indisputable facts are viewed as assumptions by other colleagues.

A simple approach to generating assumptions at the beginning of projects is assumption storming—a variation on traditional brainstorming methods. In brainstorming, teams generate as many ideas as possible in a short period of time without worrying about the quality of the ideas. In assumption storming, teams come up with as many assumptions as possible in a short period of time. After reviewing the definition of *assumption*, team members individually reflect on the problem or task they are tackling and jot down a quick list of their assumptions about the topic. Quickly going around the team, each person presents an item from his or her list, beginning with the phrase, "I assume that . . ." Each assumption is quickly recorded on the flip chart, without discussion. Once all of the assumptions are publicly posted on the flip chart, the group reviews them one at a time. It then selects the assumptions that are most critical for the team to explore, identifying specific actions that the team can take to confirm or disconfirm each assumption. Team members volunteer to take responsibility for gathering the information and reporting back to the team by a specific date.

Sometimes team members are unable to see that what they consider to be facts are in reality assumptions. In such cases the following exercise is helpful because it allows entire teams to challenge whether what individual members consider to be facts are actually facts or assumptions.

APPLICATION EXERCISE 5.2: SEPARATING ASSUMPTIONS FROM FACTS

Use the following steps to help your team separate assumptions from facts.

1. Ask the team to review the definition of an assumption.

2. Provide team members with a set of blank Post-it™ Notes. Ask team members to reflect on the problem or task they are tackling (without talking to anyone else) and quickly jot down a list of facts and assumptions about the topic. Ask members to write each item (either a fact or an assumption) on a separate Post-it™ Note.

3. Prepare a flip chart in a two-column format. Label one column "Facts—What We Know" and the other "Assumptions—What We Think We Know."

4. Ask each member of the team to select a Post-it™ Note that he or she has just filled out and read it to the team. If other team members have similar notes, they can be put together in a single string. Then ask the team to try to reach a consensus as to whether this item should be treated as a fact or as an assumption. Place the Post-it™ Note (or string of notes) in the appropriate column on the flip chart. If the team cannot reach a fairly quick consensus on whether an individual item is a fact or an assumption, place the item in the "assumption" column on the flip chart.

5. Continue the process described in the previous steps until all of the completed notes are placed on the flip chart.

   As described later in this chapter, the list of assumptions generated through this exercise will be used to plan actions the team can take to confirm or refute the validity of each assumption.

These two exercises provide ways to identify assumptions at the beginning of projects. This is important to do because it gets teams in the habit of surfacing assumptions and testing them. However, the assumptions that teams come up with at the beginning of projects are likely to be fairly obvious and superficial. Therefore, teams must continually generate assumptions throughout their projects; over the course of projects the less obvious assumptions become apparent. This was the case with the Cost Reduction Team. Only after several learning cycles did the team recognize that it was assuming that staff reductions were impossible. Even later they realized that they were avoiding making changes to their own management practices because they assumed that their past performance would be criticized.

ACTION STEP 3: ACT TO LEARN

The heart of the learning process is action. Radical teams have a bias for action, not in the sense of implementing any final solutions or recommendations but as a means of propelling team learning. The radical team approach requires that teams look at their actions in a much different way than teams traditionally have in the past. No longer is the purpose of action to execute predetermined plans. It is to learn, recognizing that the only way to transform uncertainty into certainty is through action. Radical teams take actions that will generate knowledge and test out assumptions, not to merely complete a series of tasks. When teams select actions to undertake between meetings, the actions should be selected based on their potential to produce quick new knowledge and insights. Teams should be asking themselves, "What can we do that will allow us to sit down at our next meeting and know something we do not know now?" The types of actions can vary widely. Here are some examples:

- Interview customers.
- Interview other employees.
- Obtain background briefings on related topics.
- Review records and reports.
- Meet with sponsors or champions.
- Meet with subject matter experts.
- Conduct surveys.
- Conduct focus groups.
- Visit customers.
- Tour a plant.
- Conduct a quick pilot test.
- Make a presentation and receive feedback.
- Benchmark other companies.

- Obtain information on competitors.
- Conduct a literature search.
- Search the Internet.
- Attend a seminar, conference, or training program.

These actions may not be different from those taken by traditional teams. What is different is the purpose of the actions. They are taken on the teams' behalf as a means of confirming or disconfirming assumptions and finding out things the teams do not know. As a result they are not aimed at executing predetermined plans but are intended to uncover a fundamentally new understanding of the problems at hand. Thus speed is of the essence, for it is likely that the true nature of problems will be revealed only as a result of the discoveries that emerge through action.

Some of the most powerful actions are those that involve end customers (either internal or external). Getting hard numbers regarding customers is useful when that is possible. However, statistically reliable and valid data are often not readily at hand. In these cases teams need to rely on the best available evidence. The most important test is whether the team and the key stakeholders will accept the information as valid.

Radical teams seek to take advantage of any opportunities that might exist to accelerate team learning. These happen all the time in organizations. If an opportunity is missed, it might not come along again for quite some time. For example, knowing that a major industry trade show is fast approaching, a team might come up with a way to use the trade show to gather information or test out new ideas with customers. Or recognizing that a major management meeting is coming up, the team might use this meeting as an opportunity to obtain feedback or input on the project.

The Team Learning Record presented next is a powerful tool to help project teams plan actions that will generate learning. It incorporates the assumption-surfacing methods described in the last section and takes them two steps further. First, it requires that teams explicitly list those things that are unknown to the teams but that may be important to project success. Second, it asks that teams identify the specific actions they will take to learn. This grid can also serve as a permanent record of the team learning processes. Every time teams meet, they can update the grid, with many of the items previously listed in Column 2 (what we don't know) or Column 3 (what we assume) being transferred to Column 1 (what we know). At the same time, new and subtler assumptions should appear in Column 3, initiating new rounds of action and learning. (The Team Learning Record is derived from the problem-based learning methods that were first developed to train physicians in medical schools.[4])

APPLICATION EXERCISE 5.3: TEAM LEARNING RECORD

Use the following steps to create a Team Learning Record.

Step 1: Draw the following grid on a large piece of poster paper (4'×8' is recommended).

Column 1 What We Know	Column 2 What We Don't Know	Column 3 Assumptions	Column 4 Actions to Learn

Step 2: Ask team members to jot down notes regarding items they would place in each column on the grid:

- Column 1: What We Know—things about the project that are known as facts. Objective evidence is available to prove that these items are true.

- Column 2: What We Don't Know—things about the project that we do not know and that we will need to know in order to be successful.

- Column 3: What We Assume—things that may be true but we have no objective evidence to prove it.

Step 3: Ask team members to suggest statements to be added to either the "facts" or "assumptions" column on the grid. Before writing any item on the grid, team members should challenge each other regarding whether the statement should be placed in Column 1, Column 2, or Column 3. When the team reaches consensus that an item is a fact or an assumption, write it on the grid in the appropriate column. If no consensus is reached, list the item as an assumption.

Step 4: Team members continue to suggest statements to be added to the grid, with the team deciding in which column the statement should be placed.

Step 5: Once all facts and assumptions have been listed, ask the group to begin working on Column 4: Actions to Learn. This column lists specific steps that team members will take to prove or disprove assumptions or to gather new information the team does not have. The list should include practical, short-term steps that can be quickly taken to generate new knowledge. The emphasis should be on obtaining the best available information that the team will accept as adequate support of an assumption's validity.

Step 6: Ask team members to volunteer or assign someone responsibility for gathering the information described in the "steps to learn" and to gather as much information as possible before the next meeting.

Step 7: At the next meeting ask the team to review the information gathered and what has been learned as a result.

Step 8: The process continues from meeting to meeting, with new facts and assumptions added as they arise. Over time, this process should take the form of a casual, free-flowing conversation, with team members naturally building on each other's ideas. The Team Learning Record then becomes less a structured exercise than a way to focus and summarize team discussions and actions.

ACTION STEP 4: REDUCE LEARNING CYCLE TIME

Today, when it comes to project teams, probably no topic is hotter than reducing overall project cycle time. This is especially true for new-product teams. Being six months late with a new product can cost a company 33 percent of its profits over a five-year period (Vesey, 1991). A common approach to reducing project cycle time is to devote more time and effort to planning projects. Another is to set up an accelerated schedule for completing phases of the project. Still another is to reward teams for successful completion of these projects. Unfortunately, recent research (described earlier in this book) shows that these approaches often do not produce significant reductions in cycle time (Eisenhardt and Tabrizi, 1995).

What does work is to reduce learning cycle time, which is different from project cycle time. Project cycle time is measured by calculating the total time from the beginning to the end of projects or the time needed to complete predetermined project stages. Learning cycle time has to do with how quickly teams engage in iterative learning cycles. The total number of learning cycles has been linked to how quickly new products get to market (Eisenhardt and Tabrizi, 1995) and overall team performance (Edmondson, 1999).

Team New Zealand[5]

One of the greatest sports upsets of all time occurred when Team New Zealand captured the 1995 America's Cup—only the second victory of a non-U.S. team in the yacht race's 144-year history. Not only did Team New Zealand triumph, it established a record for the greatest margin of victory, with forty-one wins and only one loss.

A major contributor to Team New Zealand's dominance was its ability to understand the learning cycle and purposefully decrease learning cycle time through a variety of innovative methods:

- The formation of a team composed of both designers and sailors at the very beginning of the project, which served as a "learning team." Together, the team engaged in rapid learning cycles, brainstorming designs, testing the designs, and reflecting on what worked and what did not work. This had never been done before by an America's Cup competitor. Usually a design team worked on the design, and the sailors implemented the design "in the water."

- The use of computer simulations to test over a thousand different designs under wave conditions that were virtually identical to those in San Diego before ever putting a boat into the water.

- The launch and test of two similar boats at the same time. Besides doubling the number of learning cycles, this made it possible to try out an innovation on one boat and use the other boat as an experimental control, which provided more usable information about what really worked.

The results of the learning process were clearly evidenced by the increasing speed of the boats in trials. Interestingly, the story of Team New Zealand helps debunk the traditional "learning curve" concept. This idea suggests that learning occurs at a rapid pace at the beginning and then tapers off, with reduced benefits over time. Instead, for Team New Zealand there was a clearly cumulative effect of learning. It was during the final learning cycles that the biggest leaps in performance occurred.

In addition, this high-speed, high-involvement team learning approach also had the benefit of ensuring the buy-in of sailors to design changes. Right up until race day, the sailors were willing to implement any changes that would make the boat go faster, even if it made their jobs more difficult.

Team New Zealand offers an example of a pattern that was evident in the radical teams that we studied: the intentional reduction of learning cycle time. The phenomenon of cumulative learning was also obvious in several teams, including the Cost Reduction Team described earlier in the chapter. It was only in the last few cycles that the Cost Reduction Team achieved the breakthroughs needed to fully reframe its project in a way that was actionable for the organization. This cumulative effect makes clear the importance of reducing learning cycle time. Without doing so, teams might never experience the learning cycles that produce the real pay-offs.

Becoming Aware of Learning Cycles

The first step in reducing learning cycle time is for teams to become aware that learning cycles exist. Most teams do not think of their projects in terms of learning cycles. They focus their attention on the meetings themselves, not on what happens between meetings. Yet from a learning perspective the work completed between meetings may be the most important element of projects because, through these actions, teams can learn.

When teams are first asked to look at their projects in terms of learning cycles, the typical response is to count the number of meetings. It makes sense to think that each meeting represents the end of one cycle and the beginning of the next (except for the first and last meetings). However, a one-to-one correspondence between meetings and cycles is rare. The majority of teams have fewer cycles than meetings. For cycles to occur, teams must take actions in between meetings and at subsequent meetings reflect on what has been learned. If teams do not enter meetings with new information or knowledge, a learning cycle has not been completed. The Cost Reduction Team was unusual in that it used just about every meeting as a means of beginning and ending a cycle.

If each meeting represents the opportunity for a new learning cycle, why do teams have fewer learning cycles than meetings? Sometimes teams end meetings without pinning down what actions will be taken between one meeting and the next. Another possibility is that members do not follow through on their commitments to take actions in between meetings. In any case it is fairly common that teams reconvene and know no more than they did at the end of the last meeting.

Figure 5.2 portrays the cycle time differences that might occur among three different teams. In this example each of the teams is locked into a schedule of bi-weekly, face-to-face meetings.

The first pattern—normal cycle time—consists of a one-on-one relationship between meetings and cycles. One cycle is completed every two weeks. The second—slow cycle time—has fewer cycles than meetings. The third—fast cycle time—has more cycles than face-to-face meetings. In the third pattern the team has found a series of creative ways to increase the number of cycles through telephone conferences and virtual meetings over the Internet.

Here is a simple way to help a team become aware of learning cycle time. Draw the three different cycle time patterns shown in Figure 5.2 on a flip chart. Then as a group discuss which pattern most resembles the team's learning cycle time: the normal pattern (an equal number of meetings and cycles), the slow pattern (fewer cycles than meetings), or the fast pattern (intentionally increasing the number of cycles over that which might occur through a regular schedule of meetings).

An activity such as this is best done when teams are about one-third of the way through their projects. They can then plan actions to reduce learning cycle time and later in the project (about two-thirds of the way through) repeat the process. Teams characterized as having slow cycle times can take steps to make sure that each meeting represents the start of a new cycle. Teams that have normal cycle times can look at ways to accelerate the number of cycles.

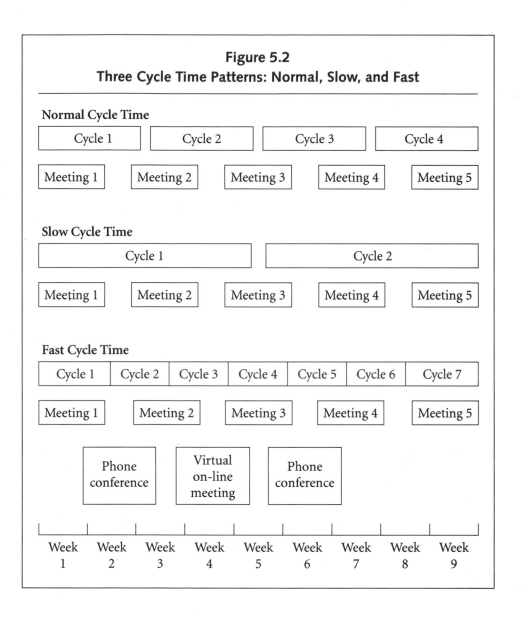

Figure 5.2
Three Cycle Time Patterns: Normal, Slow, and Fast

Normal Cycle Time

| Cycle 1 | Cycle 2 | Cycle 3 | Cycle 4 |

| Meeting 1 | Meeting 2 | Meeting 3 | Meeting 4 | Meeting 5 |

Slow Cycle Time

| Cycle 1 | Cycle 2 |

| Meeting 1 | Meeting 2 | Meeting 3 | Meeting 4 | Meeting 5 |

Fast Cycle Time

| Cycle 1 | Cycle 2 | Cycle 3 | Cycle 4 | Cycle 5 | Cycle 6 | Cycle 7 |

| Meeting 1 | Meeting 2 | Meeting 3 | Meeting 4 | Meeting 5 |

Phone conference | Virtual on-line meeting | Phone conference

Week 1 | Week 2 | Week 3 | Week 4 | Week 5 | Week 6 | Week 7 | Week 8 | Week 9

The following are some possible ways to reduce learning cycle time:

- *Find creative alternatives to face-to-face meetings.* Because the beginning and end of cycles require the collective presence of the entire team, a major impediment to reducing cycle time is the difficulty of holding face-to-face team meetings. Rather than wait for face-to-face meetings, many teams accelerate learning cycles through telephone conferences or videoconferences. In addition, a great deal of information can be passed electronically among team members through the use of groupware or by sending e-mail messages. (Caution: while electronic exchanges can expedite the overall process, they are not substitutes for whole team meetings at the beginning and end of cycles.)

- *Hold mini-meetings.* Many teams call these stand-up meetings. They should not last more than ten or fifteen minutes. These meetings are useful to follow up on actions that should be occurring between regular meetings. For example, let us say that team members plan to conduct a series of interviews over the two weeks, between face-to-face meetings. The team might agree to hold a stand-up meeting after a week to make any needed adjustments and to make sure that the team walks into the next meeting with valuable information.

- *Complete between-meeting tasks.* Team members need to make sure that assigned tasks are completed between meetings. Otherwise teams will reconvene without the information needed to complete one learning cycle and move on to the next.

- *Conduct parallel experiments.* Complete two cycles at the same time. This technique is at the heart of the "skunk works" method of product development, credited with bringing the personal computer to market. Skunk works involves setting up multiple teams to tackle the same project. Each team is kept separate from the others and ignorant of what the others are doing. Through this method multiple approaches are tested out quickly, with the final design often being a combination of the separate experiments. A single project team can use the same idea. For example, let us say that your company is holding a series of regional sales meetings over a two-week period. Team members could go to different meetings and try out different approaches and then return to the team. For all practical purposes, two learning cycles were completed at the same time.

- *Summarize information in a usable fashion.* Teams often slow down because information gathered between meetings is not summarized and presented to the teams in a usable fashion. For example, let us say that a team has distributed a survey questionnaire to fifty individuals and the team is reconvening to review the results of the questionnaire. In order for the team as a whole to complete Step 4: Reflect and Learn, the survey results need to be summarized and distributed to team members in advance of the meeting so everyone can come to the meeting ready to share perceptions regarding what the questionnaire results tell them.

APPLICATION EXERCISE 5.4: KEEPING A LEARNING CYCLE RECORD

After your team has been operating for a while, suggest that this might be a useful time to take a look at your learning cycles.

1. Draw a table like the one shown:

Learning Cycles	Actions Taken	What Was Learned
1		
2		
3		
4		
(Add more cycles as needed.)		

2. As a whole team discuss the following questions:

What have we done so far that has helped to speed up our learning cycles?

In retrospect, what might we have done that would have served to speed up our learning cycles? In other words, what could we have done so that, sitting here today, we would have completed a greater number of learning cycles?

Looking ahead, what might we do to accelerate the speed of our learning?

3. Throughout the project periodically suggest that the team update its learning map and again discuss the questions in item 2.

Figure 5.3 presents an example of what a learning cycle record might look like for the Cost Reduction Team described at the beginning of this chapter.

Figure 5.3
Learning Cycle Record: Cost Reduction Team

Learning Cycles	Actions Taken	What Was Learned
1	Investigated use of modified voltage transformers: where they are currently being used and opportunities for additional use. Held general brainstorming sessions about cost reduction ideas.	Modified voltage transformers are used just about everywhere that is feasible. There appear to be many other possible ways to reduce costs.
2	Selected ideas from brainstorming sessions that looked most feasible and investigated them.	Estimated total cost reduction is 10%—short of 20% goal.
3	Updated sponsor.	Need to find at least another 10%; should consider labor reduction possibilities; should look further for cost reductions.
4	Developed some additional cost savings ideas and discussed with union representatives.	Union receptive as long as labor reductions comply with contract provisions; should achieve 20% cost reduction but may take a few years to obtain full amount.
5	Went back to original list of ideas and investigated some ideas that were discarded as not feasible.	Some basic practices could be changed to produce another 10%, for a 30% total.
6	Worked out details of implementing full set of recommendations and developed proposal for presentation to senior management.	Presentation made and accepted by senior management.

ACTION STEP 5: IMPROVE THE LEARNING PROCESS

Reducing learning cycle time is not enough to increase the speed of learning. Radical teams also give attention to the quality of their learning and the effectiveness with which they complete each step in the learning cycle. They periodically stop to review how well they are learning and take actions to improve their learning. This constitutes the highest form of learning: learning to learn. Through this process teams become critically aware of their own learning process and, over the course of their projects, develop the capability to learn more effectively.

Using Ground Rules to Improve Team Learning

Traditionally, one of the common ways that teams improve their effectiveness is to establish ground rules that describe how they would like to operate. Typically, team ground rules deal with the basics of effective meeting management and group communications, covering issues such as starting and ending meetings on time, keeping discussions on track, listening to fellow team members, and sticking to agendas. In most cases teams establish ground rules at the beginning of their projects and periodically stop during projects to see how well they are following those rules. Over time, teams' original ground rules become part of their unstated norms and are no longer needed.

This same process can be used to improve team learning. However, the ground rules need to cover team behaviors that are most critical for enhancing the team learning process, not just meeting management and communications. Figure 5.4 shows how the ground rules that radical teams set need to be substantially different from those set by traditional teams.

Although the substance of the ground rules needs to be different, the rules themselves can be used in much the same way: to structure debriefing sessions at the end of team meetings that can be used to assess and plan actions to improve team effectiveness. In this way radical teams are continuously in the process of getting better at their own learning.

Using Learning Styles to Improve Team Learning

Another way to improve the quality of team learning is to become aware of learning styles and how they influence team effectiveness. As used here, *team learning style* refers to the degree to which teams prefer certain steps in the learning cycle to other steps in the learning cycle. As shown in Figure 5.5, it is possible to iden-

Figure 5.4
Examples of Traditional and Radical Team Ground Rules

Traditional Team Ground Rules	Radical Team Ground Rules
• Establish or review the team's goal and purpose.	• Start from the position of "I don't know," not "I know."
• Get group agreement on an agenda.	• Pose questions rather than provide solutions.
• Clarify roles (facilitator, recorder, reporter).	• Explicitly state any assumptions you hold.
• Listen actively to whoever is speaking.	• Guide others to separate assumptions from facts.
• Allow equal "air time." Encourage everyone to participate.	• Be curious—willing to explore topics and areas that may or may not prove to be relevant.
• Use time efficiently; avoid getting sidetracked on peripheral issues.	• Identify quick actions that will likely generate the most learning.
• Seek to reach consensus decisions that everyone can support.	• Challenge the group to speed up its learning (meet sooner or use phone conferences, e-mail, or videoconferences).
• Summarize decisions and assign responsibilities for carrying them out.	• Restate or reword the problem if it doesn't make sense any more.

tify four different learning styles that seem to correspond to the four steps in the learning cycle model used throughout this book.

Framing-oriented teams spend considerable time and energy understanding and defining their projects. They strive for high levels of certainty regarding the project goals, the desired final outcomes, and the key milestones that need to be reached along the way. They want to obtain as much background information as possible, even if they are not exactly sure how such information might be useful. They want to understand how their projects fit into the larger picture, such as company business goals or other related initiatives. They want to look at their projects from all angles. Framing-oriented teams may find it hard to deal with ambiguity and changes

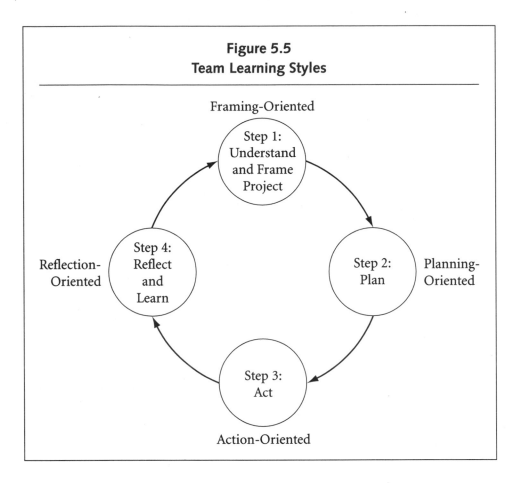

Figure 5.5
Team Learning Styles

Framing-Oriented

Step 1:
Understand
and Frame
Project

Step 4:
Reflect
and
Learn

Reflection-
Oriented

Step 2:
Plan

Planning-
Oriented

Step 3:
Act

Action-Oriented

in direction. They can get hung up on theoretical discussions and abstract theorizing about issues that might more easily be resolved through quick action.

Planning-oriented teams seek to thoroughly work out the details and specifics of how projects will be managed and how any actions will be implemented. They tend to develop detailed project plans. They keep discussions short and to the point, and they have little tolerance for theoretical discussions and digressions. They can jump to conclusions early in projects and not examine all the possibilities. They also have a tendency to get hung up on minor and irrelevant details.

Action-oriented teams tackle their projects as a trial-and-error learning process. Their tendency is to experiment and jump into action, sometimes without having a clear sense of what they are trying to do. When things do not work out as planned, they chalk it up to experience. As a result they may waste time and effort when both could have been saved with more thoughtful planning. Although they might believe in trial-and-error learning, they are often so action-oriented that they find it hard to stop in order to reflect and learn from their own experiences.

Reflection-oriented teams spend a great deal of time reviewing and interpreting the meaning of events that have occurred, information the team has gathered, and actions the team has taken. Reflection-oriented teams avoid jumping to conclusions and try to avoid tight deadlines. They tend to be very aware of their own processes and frequently stop and review how they are working together as a team. Reflection-oriented teams have a tendency to overanalyze and make situations more complicated than they need to be.

Here are four guidelines to improve team learning styles:

Seek Balance. Radical teams are able to get around learning cycles quickly and effectively. To accomplish this, it is important that teams seek some balance among the four possible team learning styles. Teams need to be skilled at each step of the learning cycle and spend just enough time and energy on each step before moving on to the next.

Know When a Strength Becomes a Weakness. Any of the four learning styles can be overdone. A team might be very good at planning and have the tendency to spend meeting after meeting working out detailed project plans. Such a planning-oriented team might overemphasize this step of the cycle at the expense of the other steps, designing elaborate project plans without ever checking out whether the assumptions the plans are based on make sense or not. Therefore, it is important that teams discuss their predisposition to get hung up on one or more steps of the cycle and keep an eye on this tendency throughout their projects.

Go Against the Grain. At the same time, you can increase your effectiveness by consciously picking out one of your team's weakest learning styles and purposefully seek to go against the grain, that is, to intentionally spend time and effort on a step in the learning cycle that you might have neglected otherwise. For example, a team that spends very little time reflecting might purposefully set the goal of improving its skill and increasing its effort related to this step in the cycle.

Adapt to the Needs of Your Projects. Teams also need to be flexible when it comes to learning styles. Overall, some projects might require more work on one step of the learning cycle than another. For example, some projects might demand that teams engage in a great deal of action and experimentation, whereas others require more focus on planning. The demands might also vary for different stages in the learning cycle. For example, Step 3 might be more important earlier in the project than later.

Typically, it takes some time for team learning styles to become evident, especially if it is the first time the team members have worked together. One practical way to introduce learning styles at the beginning of projects is to give members a chance to explore and share their personal learning styles with each other. Identifying personal learning styles is a great team-building exercise and helps teams understand the idea of learning cycles at a gut level rather than just intellectually. Probably the best way to identify personal learning styles is through the use of a commercially available instrument such as the *Learning Styles Questionnaire* (Honey and Mumford, 1995b).[6] The precise names of the four styles described in this questionnaire are a little different from the one used in this book. However, they are based on the same underlying concepts, and people usually have no problems going back and forth from one set of terms to the other.

After each person fills out a questionnaire and analyzes the results, it is often useful to create a summary profile of the entire team that lists each team member's most preferred and least preferred style. The team can then discuss how the team's particular mixture of learning styles might apply to the project. For example, how might the learning styles help or hurt the team as it proceeds with the project? Also, team members might make agreements to help each other go against the grain and work to build up their least preferred learning styles. For example, a team member who often jumps into action without sufficient planning might ask another team member, one whose strong suit is planning, to provide feedback and coaching throughout the project to help build up his or her planning-oriented style. Some teams keep their personal learning styles visibly posted throughout their projects as a constant reminder of their preferences.

As projects progress, each team's unique learning style profile emerges. It is reflected in the collective actions of the team. In most cases it corresponds to the predominant personal learning styles of members, but this is not always true. I have seen teams made up of the same members exhibit different learning styles with different projects. Therefore, it is often helpful if teams stop and discuss their overall team learning styles at key points in their projects.

The following is an exercise that can be used to generate discussion regarding team learning styles. It is best used after a team has had the opportunity to work together for a period of time.

APPLICATION EXERCISE 5.5: LEARNING STYLES

Listed next are several common practices of project teams.

Step 1: Think about the practices of your team so far in this project. Select the five practices that your team engages in most frequently and the five practices that your team engages in least frequently. Place an "X" after each of the ten statements in the appropriate right-hand column. Place exactly five "X"s in the "Most Frequent" column and five in the "Least Frequent" column.

Team Practices	Five Most Frequent	Five Least Frequent
Our team:		
1. Conducts quick experiments.		
2. Makes sure at the outset that all team members fully understand the purpose of the project.		
3. Develops an overall project plan with time lines.		
4. Objectively analyzes new information that is available to the team as the project progresses.		
5. Obtains general background information about the project.		
6. Fully works out the details regarding how the team's recommendations will be implemented.		
7. Stops periodically to explore the differing perspectives of team members about how the project is going.		
8. Takes advantage of opportunities that arise, even if they were not part of the original project plan.		
9. Uses project tools (like Gantt charts, critical path analysis, and others) to sequence the project.		
10. Redefines the nature and scope of the project whenever needed.		
11. Examines problems and roadblocks that have arisen in the project.		
12. Takes initial steps that will help tell the team what to do next.		

Team Practices	Five Most Frequent	Five Least Frequent
Our team:		
13. Gathers information to see if team members' ideas and hunches are valid.		
14. Anticipates potential future problems with implementing the project that might arise.		
15. Reviews how well the team has worked together and how it might work together even better in the future.		
16. Thinks about all of the possible alternative approaches to the project that might exist.		

Step 2: As a team, combine the responses of individual team members on a single summary sheet by tallying the total number of "most" and "least" responses for each item, as they correspond to the four learning styles shown next. List the total number of "most" responses in the "most" column and the total number of "least" responses in the "least" column:

Step in Learning Cycle	Team Learning Style	Items	Total Number of "Most" Responses	Total Number of "Least" Responses
Step 1: Understand and Frame	Framing-oriented	2, 5, 10, 16		
Step 2: Plan	Planning-oriented	3, 6, 9, 14		
Step 3: Act	Action-oriented	1, 8, 12, 13		
Step 4: Reflect and Learn	Reflection-oriented	4, 7, 11, 15		

Step 3: As a team, discuss the following questions and how they apply to your team:

Which learning style or styles do we tend to most prefer as a team? How might this preference affect the overall success of our project?

At what phases in our project will our learning style preferences help us the most? At what phases will our preferences help us the least?

What specific roadblocks and problems might occur as a result of our learning styles, and how might we overcome them?

Which of the learning styles should we spend less time and effort on as the project proceeds? What specific actions will we take to do this?

Which of the learning styles should we spend more time and effort on as the project proceeds? What specific actions will we take to do this?

This chapter presented five action steps for increasing the speed of learning of project teams:

Action Step 1: Acknowledge uncertainty and the need to learn.

Action Step 2: Separate facts from assumptions.

Action Step 3: Act to learn.

Action Step 4: Reduce learning cycle time.

Action Step 5: Improve team learning.

The next chapter presents five action steps for increasing the depth of learning.

Breakthrough
Action Steps to Increase the Depth of Team Learning

What we did was a lot of reflective stuff. That's where we became confused. Was it to get this project completed or to do a whole lot of reflecting? We felt [that all of this reflecting] was slowing us down, and we didn't understand why we needed to do this at this point. We were concerned how we were going to complete the project on time if we were doing all this reflecting and talking to each other.

From a project team member's log

The last chapter dealt with how to increase the speed of team learning. This chapter presents a series of action steps designed to produce project breakthroughs by enhancing the depth of learning:

Action Step 1: Make it safe.

Action Step 2: Detect early warning signs.

Action Step 3: Explore divergent views.

Action Step 4: Exploit breakdowns to produce breakthroughs.

Action Step 5: Capture lessons learned from cycle to cycle.

Action Step 6: Reframe projects to reflect deepening understandings.

The depth of learning is determined by the degree to which teams are able to reflect on information and knowledge acquired as projects progress, create new common understandings, and as a result, reframe their projects when warranted.

Our studies of the project teams described earlier raised several critical questions related to increasing depth:

- Why do teams frequently ignore concrete and objective information that contradicts previous assumptions about the project?
- Why are teams often unable to change course despite all of the evidence that they should?
- Why does it take months, sometimes even years, before all team members come to a conclusion that somebody on their team had been able to reach at the very first meeting?

Some insights into these questions are provided by the story of the Cochlear Implant Team.

The Cochlear Implant Team[1]

In the late 1970s the health services division of a leading high-technology research and development company began exploring a revolutionary product idea: cochlear implants. Cochlear implants are surgically implanted hearing aids that the company felt had the potential to provide the profoundly deaf with the ability to hear sound for the first time. A steering committee was formed to head up the project, and a research team was assembled to begin the work. The goal was to be the first to market cochlear implants. At that time no competitor was known to be considering introducing cochlear implants. The team enjoyed *carte blanche* in terms of resources and corporate support.

As the project began, the steering committee was faced with a critical decision: Should the company pursue a single-channel device, a multichannel device, or both? The committee, at its earliest meetings, seemed to lean toward the single-channel device. The hunch was that safety considerations during surgery would constitute the major obstacle to obtaining widespread acceptance of the new product. Compared to multichannel devices, the single-channel device had a shorter stem and therefore should present less of a safety risk. Also, the single-channel device was simpler and should be faster to get to market.

The steering committee decided to move full steam ahead toward becoming the first to market a simple, single-channel implant. Multichannel implants, although still a possibility in the future, would be put on the back burner and reconsidered as part of a second generation of products. FDA approval for the single-channel implant was quickly obtained, and soon over fifty people were working full-time on the project, with an annual budget of $6 million.

Within a few months, the company was surprised to hear that a major competitor was also moving ahead with cochlear implants and was using a multichannel device. The FDA had approved the multichannel device with no apparent concern for the supposed increased safety risks inherent with a multichannel product. In fact, the other company began promoting the superiority of multichannel implants in producing clearer recognition of everyday speech patterns.

The committee responded to competitor claims. It highlighted the safety superiority of single-channel devices and cited studies showing that single-channel devices produced more natural environmental sounds. Research aimed at supporting the safety of single-channel devices was increased. Plans to introduce multichannel implants in later generations of products were abandoned, with full effort given to further enhancing the safety advantage of single-channel products. The steering committee was convinced that, once full tests of the implants with real patients occurred, the single-channel devices would be shown to be markedly superior.

Over the next several years, more and more evidence accumulated in favor of multichannel devices. Independent researchers began publishing studies showing that multichannel implants performed much better than did single-channel implants. Market surveys reported that potential customers might hold back on purchasing the company's product and wait for multichannel devices to become available. In response the company revised its sales and revenue projections downward. Single-channel devices would capture less of the primary market, and it would take longer to get its share of the market than previous projections had indicated. For the first time the company began raising concerns about the profitability of the project and began questioning expenses.

In response the project team changed its basic strategy. It decided to expand the target market beyond the profoundly deaf to include those with mild-to-moderate hearing impairments. This decision dramatically increased the potential sales of the product and, at least for a time, held off concerns about the single-channel device's inferiority. A single-channel device should be perfect for this market because safety was of more concern than quality. Single-channel implants could become the preferred choice of the majority of hearing aid wearers because of convenience and appearance.

Yet more and more evidence piled up showing that the single-channel product had problems. Both the FDA and the National Institutes of Health released studies reporting that multichannel devices produced much better sound and did not pose a safety risk. In 1985, the company installed a new project manager who was asked to reexamine the commercial and technical viability of the product and to recommend whether to continue or abandon the project.

Over the next few years, corporate resources devoted to the project dissipated as the Cochlear Implant Project continued to flounder. Eleven years after the project started, and after several million dollars had been invested, the company abandoned cochlear implants and sold the rights of the Cochlear Implant Project to the competition.

Imagine that you are a member of the steering committee for the Cochlear Implant Project. At your monthly meetings evidence accrues indicating that the team is headed down the wrong path. There is mounting evidence that single-channel devices are neither technologically superior nor safer. Yet the team continues to hold on to its original assumption: that a single-channel device is safer than and of equal quality to multichannel devices. The committee even gives the project more money and more people to prove that your approach is right. Why didn't somebody say something? What were you thinking?

Our study of twenty teams provided a unique opportunity to understand why teams sometimes act as the steering committee did in the Cochlear Implant Team. Members of many of the teams were asked to keep personal logs throughout their projects, recording their private thoughts about what was going on with their teams. We even stopped in meetings and had people make entries in their logs. At the end of the projects, researchers reviewed the logs. What we found was that many, many times team members were saying one thing to their teams and something quite different in their logs. For example, at a team's first meeting, one person made the following note: "I felt so wimpy. I didn't understand why we were doing what we were doing. But I didn't say anything." Almost two months later, exasperated by the team's lack of progress, she finally shared her feelings.

This phenomenon occurred so frequently and was so pervasive that it led to the following generalization: *In almost all cases and at almost all times, somebody on the team is questioning the team's direction, and these concerns are never voiced to the team.*

Based on this observation, anyone watching a team in action can reasonably infer that there is at least one person, if not more, who is sitting at the table with sincere and deep concerns about where the team is headed but who is not voicing those concerns. These team members are thinking one thing but probably saying something different to the team. Why? One factor is "group think" (Janis, 1982). Group think refers to the tendency for team members to go along with a group decision, even if they are totally convinced that it is the wrong way to go. In fact, it sometimes turns out that none of the members in the group really backed the decision—they just thought everyone else did. As a result a whole group might make a decision with which nobody really agrees.

Consider the ramifications for your own teams. The next time you are sitting around a conference table and looking your colleagues in the eyes, there is a great chance that at least one person is totally convinced that the team is misdirected. (In fact, sometimes you are the person feeling that way.) Yet these conclusions or, more important, the information that leads to them is never voiced to the team. As a result teams miss key opportunities to consider the potential for reframing its project. There is a good chance that this explains what happened with the Cochlear Implant Team.

Radical teams work hard to increase the likelihood of reframing, avoiding the tendency to miss signs that they need to change their fundamental understandings of their projects. This chapter describes several action steps that radical teams take to continue to enhance the depth of learning.

ACTION STEP 1: MAKE IT SAFE

According to several studies (Schein, 1993; Edmondson, 1999), the single most critical factor determining how well teams learn is whether team members and other stakeholders feel that it is safe to

- Speak what's on their minds.
- Admit mistakes and errors.
- Acknowledge that they do not have the answers and do not know what to do.
- Ask for assistance.
- Question original goals.
- Challenge management direction.

Teams will go to great lengths to avoid any embarrassment or threat; moreover, they will cover up the fact that they are doing so (Argyris and Schön, 1996). That explains why teams such as the Cochlear Implant Team engage in a sustained conspiracy of silence in the face of mounting contradictory evidence.

Radical teams work hard to create an environment in which members feel safe. The first step in establishing such a climate is committing to the learning and discovery process described in the previous chapter. This creates an overall context where acknowledging that "I don't know" is not only accepted but is expected. Moreover, "making it safe" creates a "practice field" where teams can experiment and learn together.

The degree of safety that exists is influenced by factors external to the team. For example, the coaching provided by sponsors, champions, and other organizational leaders is key. Moreover, the degree to which support and resources are provided by the organization is important. These topics are covered in more detail in Chapter Eight.

Teams can do a lot throughout their projects to build and maintain high levels of safety. Here is a great illustration.

The Mathematics Improvement Team

One of the most successful teams that we studied was the Mathematics Improvement Team in an elementary school. The team produced phenomenal results. Student math scores on the state's standardized test jumped 65 percent over a three-year period. To achieve these results, the team needed to confront a potentially embarrassing fact: most teachers did not have the basic knowledge of mathematics principles needed to teach effectively. Not only did the team make this discovery, it allowed for everyone involved to take the steps needed to remedy the situation without losing face or being threatened in any way. Here is how it happened:

Cycle 1: A team was formed made up of three teachers, a parent, and an administrator. (Several other teachers in the grades targeted for improvement were not on the team.) The team studied available research on teaching elementary school mathematics and visited a similar school in another district that had made great gains in mathematics. Evidence suggested that the teachers needed to teach math using a hands-on, problem-solving process. This technique is an alternative to the traditional drill-and-practice method. It has students use tangible objects to develop an understanding of basic math concepts and emphasizes problem solving using real-world problems. This method teaches students to understand the underlying principles rather than rely on mathematical formulas. As a result students discover that there is almost always more than one path to the right answer.

Cycle 2: The team interviewed all of the school's teachers to find out if they were currently using hands-on, problem-solving methods. Responses varied. A few teachers said they were using problem-solving teaching methods, as much as they had time for. Others said they did not have sufficient teaching materials to teach math using this method.

Cycle 3: The team decided to try a two-pronged approach: (1) making sure the teachers had the materials needed to teach hands-on math and (2) providing training so teachers felt comfortable using hands-on, problem-solving teaching methods. The team began to look for someone to provide staff development. The district had a math curriculum expert who could provide the training. However, the teachers decided they wanted to go with someone from outside the district. They selected a professor who had written an article the team had read and who was working with the teachers in the school they had visited.

Cycle 4: At this point the team became confused. When preparing to order instructional materials, members found full, unopened boxes of materials that had been sent over by the district's central office the previous year. In addition, the training appeared to have done little good. Teachers continued to teach using the old methods, citing various reasons such as, "I'm swamped. I just don't have time to spend more time preparing to teach each day." The team asked the professor, who had been well received by the teachers, to stop in and observe the classrooms to see what was going on. The teachers said they would have no problem as long as the professor made only a summary report back to the team and did not describe what specific teachers did in their classrooms.

Cycle 5: The professor reported back that, on the whole, only a small portion of class time was being spent on math, and most of that time was being used for traditional drill and practice. She also observed that on those rare occasions when problem-solving methods were being used, they were often used incorrectly. Many teachers corrected students who came up with the right answers but did so using different problem-solving strategies than what the teachers used. During this conversation one of the math teachers who was on the team casually commented: "You know, I was never that good in math in school." Everyone laughed. Several people shared stories of the tough times they had had learning math in school. The professor gently suggested that maybe the teachers could use a mathematics refresher. The team concluded that it would offer small-group coaching sessions to the teachers, with just two or three teachers at a time.

Cycle 6: The teachers, on the whole, welcomed the idea of small-group coaching sessions, responding, "I'm sure I can pick up a tip or two." During these sessions the professor subtly covered some of the underlying math principles needed to teach using these methods. When needed, she would go into the teachers' classrooms and demonstrate specific techniques. The word came back, both from the professor and the teachers on the team: progress was being made. Teachers were using the hands-on, problem-solving methods and, just as important, they were devoting more classroom time to teaching math.

Cycle 7: At the end of the school year the team asked the teachers for recommendations regarding what additional help they would like in the future. Overwhelmingly, the teachers asked that the coaching sessions continue when school resumed in the fall. The professor came back to the school and held coaching sessions for the next two school years. During that time teachers appeared to get better and better using the hands-on, problem-solving teaching methods. Students' scores in mathematics jumped from fourteenth to second out of the fifteen other schools in the district.

What makes this team's story so enlightening are the subtle ways that the team made it safe for everyone—both team members and others who were not on the team—to admit that they were not fully knowledgeable and needed help from others. In this school, like many others, there had been a "norm of privacy" in which what occurs in classrooms, once the doors are shut, is up to individual teachers. From this perspective everyone is respected as a professional, and there is a recognition that different educators can get results using different methods. Here the team broke through the long-standing wall of privacy and professional courtesy relatively quickly. How did they do it? The team gave the teachers control over several core decisions in the process, including who would provide staff development and how it would occur. It engaged in probes that allowed people to take controlled risks at early stages and see what happened as a result. It provided needed help and resources so people could feel they had a good shot at being successful.

The following are some specific guidelines you can use to establish a climate of safety with your teams.

Set Ground Rules and Norms

Set ground rules and establish norms to create a safe environment. Throughout their projects, teams need to work to establish norms for behavior that encourage being open, taking risks, challenging the status quo, questioning team direction, and making errors. As described in the last chapter, the creation of norms can be helped by setting ground rules for behaviors at the beginning of projects and then periodically reviewing how well the team is following them. These ground rules can be very simple:

- There are no dumb ideas.
- Be willing to take risks.
- State what's on your mind.
- Respect ideas other than your own.

However, establishing these as ground rules is a meaningless exercise if they are not translated into action by the team, which should be a continuous process that is worked at throughout your projects. Try the following:

- Stop at the end of meetings and invite the team to review how well they are following the norms.
- Call attention to ground rules at key times in meetings. This is best done at a point when someone on the team has just exhibited the desired behavior, such

as taking a risk or expressing a potentially embarrassing idea or fact. This can be done very naturally by saying something like, "We've been talking about taking risks, and this provides a great example of what it means to take a risk." You might also mention the ground rules when you believe they are not being followed: "One of our ground rules is that there are no dumb ideas. It seems as if we dismissed some ideas pretty quickly here. What does everyone else think?"

• Establish new ground rules as needed during the project to focus on specific issues that have arisen.

• Yield control. Allow those at risk to control potentially risky situations. People feel a lot safer if they are in control of their own destinies. Think about any time that you go swimming in cold water. You feel a lot better if you do it at your own speed and in your own way. The Mathematics Improvement Team did a great job of this, involving the math teachers in the decision regarding how and when to do staff development and who would do it.

• Test assumptions. Test risk-related assumptions as quickly as possible. But let us not be naive. Many times it is not safe for teams to challenge management, openly express viewpoints, or acknowledge mistakes. The best way to deal with safety-related concerns is to treat them like any other assumptions teams might have about their projects—test them out as quickly as possible.

For example, a team charged with investigating whether there are some potential uses for the by-products of its core products identified the following risk-related assumptions at its first meeting:

- Somebody already has "the answer." This is just an exercise to prove that they are right.

- There are boundaries we don't know about.

- Any approach that would really work will be cost prohibitive.

- The numbers that we have been given about market size and market share are likely inaccurate. Nobody really knows the true numbers.

- We will not receive the support we need from the business managers who are responsible for these product areas.

The team felt that it was possibly being set up to fail with a bogus project, the real aim of which was to provide political cover for a senior executive. Before going

...am requested to meet with the division vice pres-
...rs to see if any or all of the assumptions were

...out and directly ask, "Are we being set up on
...a a series of carefully structured questions that would
...ut what they needed to know:

- Has this been looked into in the past? If so, what was found out?
- What types of return-on-investment hurdles must this project make to be approved?
- How prepared is the organization to do what it takes to make this project work?
- What is the role of the business managers in this project? What types of support will they be able to provide for the project?

The team was encouraged when it found out that the company was serious about investigating these new products and that most of the assumptions were not true. In a few cases the team decided to keep an eye on the assumptions as the project progressed. By checking out the assumptions, not only did the team feel better about the project but it laid the groundwork with the division vice president and the business managers to get the support that would be needed later in the project.

Increase Risks Gradually

Gradually increase risks over the course of projects. You cannot expect anyone to immediately take significant risks at the beginning of projects. It took quite some time for the teachers on the Mathematics Improvement Team to acknowledge that they were never very good at math. Similarly, in last chapter's Cost Reduction Team it took the managers almost the entire project to consider the possibility that they might need to change some of their own management practices.

Yet the radical teams we observed gradually raised the temperature on issues so that more and more risks were taken as projects progressed. The following is a simple yet powerful exercise you can use to illustrate the need for people to consider making personal changes and taking personal risks in order to achieve desired project results.[2]

APPLICATION EXERCISE 6.1: CLOSER TO HOME

Use the following steps to help team members accept the need for personal change.

Step 1: Each team member generates a list of potential ideas or solutions to a problem or issue.

Step 2: Each person separates the list into two categories: (1) those that require others to change and (2) those that require that he or she change personally. In most cases the lists primarily consist of things for other people to do.

Step 3: The whole group discusses the differences between the two lists and the natural tendency for people to avoid ideas and suggestions that require personal change. The team then explores the ramifications of this to the project and what can be done to increase the degree to which people will be open to making the personal changes needed to produce desired results.

ACTION STEP 2: DETECT EARLY WARNING SIGNS

Radical teams are driven by a search for objective information that can be confirmed or disconfirmed through action. In many cases there are signs very early in projects that teams may be headed in the wrong direction. That was certainly the case with the Cochlear Implant Team. There was unmistakable evidence that the single-channel approach was doomed from the beginning, but the team ignored the evidence. Many of the teams we studied followed this same pattern. It was rare that teams, on obtaining early contradictory evidence, considered the possibility that the assumptions framing their approach may have been faulty. There are several likely reasons for this. At early stages of projects, information suggesting that teams are heading down the wrong path is often ambiguous and difficult to detect. Moreover, team members are still getting to know each other, and a climate of safety and trust has not yet developed. Also there is often a feeling that the team has plenty of time and there is comparatively little pressure for results.

Yet it only gets tougher to challenge assumptions as time goes on. The longer projects continue, the more of a cumulative investment there is. Therefore, at later stages in projects it will likely take more and more evidence on the other side of the scale to cause project teams to write off the dollars already invested and change course. Team members often have strong psychological investments in the success of their projects. Personal stakes are often involved, affecting professional reputations and career advancement.

One way for team members to increase their sensitivity to early warning signals is to keep personal learning logs throughout their projects. Many people initially resist the idea of keeping logs but later appreciate their usefulness in helping them be aware of what is occurring with their projects. Originally, our research team asked team members to keep personal logs as a way to help us gather research data. We soon realized that team members were using the logs as tools for personal reflection. In some teams the team as a whole used the logs during meetings to help them reflect on their projects. Here are some suggestions regarding how you might use a personal log with a project.

APPLICATION EXERCISE 6.2A: PERSONAL LEARNING LOG

Every few days, or any time something significant occurs related to the project, spend five to ten minutes thinking about the following questions. Then jot down your thoughts in your log.

- Overall, how do you feel about the team's direction?
- What objective data and information do you have to suggest the team is headed in the right direction?
- What objective data and information do you have to suggest the team is headed in the wrong direction?
- Have there been any surprises, roadblocks, or disappointments? If so, what were they and what do you think they might mean to the project?
- If, later on in the project, the team is blindsided by something unexpected, what might that be?
- To what degree have you explicitly shared these perceptions (your responses to the previous questions) with your team?
- How do you think your fellow team members are feeling about the team's direction? What perceptions do other team members have that you suspect they may not be sharing with the team?

If all team members keep personal learning logs, the logs can also be used periodically during team meetings as follows:

Step 1: The team should allow five to ten minutes for members to silently reflect on the questions listed and make notes in their logs.

Step 2: One by one, team members should share their perceptions with each other.

Step 3: When individuals present what is in their logs, it is important that other team members limit their comments to asking clarification questions. They should not agree or disagree with others' viewpoints. They should just try to understand.

Step 4: After all team members have had a chance to express what they wrote in their logs, the team should explore what these perceptions mean for the project.

The Ladder of Inference[3]

Sticking to the facts is harder to do than it sounds. The human mind makes meaning by taking limited information, interpreting what this information means, making some conclusions, and determining an appropriate course of action as a result. We all do it so often and so fast that we are not even aware we are doing it. Chris Argyris (1993) uses the analogy of walking up a ladder to explain this process. The bottom rung of the ladder is the objective information that the team has available to it. Each subsequent rung up the ladder is made of the interpretation and conclusions that are drawn from the objective information. The final rung is the team's decisions regarding what it believes needs to be done.

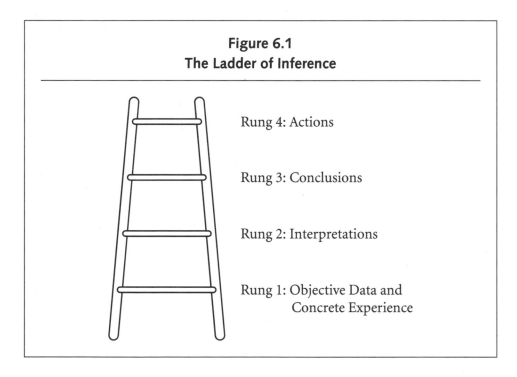

Figure 6.1
The Ladder of Inference

Rung 4: Actions

Rung 3: Conclusions

Rung 2: Interpretations

Rung 1: Objective Data and
Concrete Experience

During typical team conversations, members have already walked up their own ladders of inference. Then, perched on the top of their ladders, they try to convince others that they have drawn the right conclusions and persuade others what should be done as a result. In contrast, radical teams strive to walk up each rung of the ladder together. They try to work from a foundation of objective information and data. Members seek to build their conclusions together from the ground up. Even more important, team members try to free themselves from their preconceived notions and perspectives, present the objective information they feel is relevant, and then carefully offer their own interpretations of the data. They invite other team members to confirm or disconfirm the conclusions that are drawn. At the same time, team members ask questions to understand how others are interpreting information.

APPLICATION EXERCISE 6.2B: LADDER OF INFERENCE

This exercise is best used at a point when the team has just gathered some information critical to your project through conversations with subject matter experts, customers, senior managers, or other key individuals. It is great if there is an audiotape or written transcript of the conversations.

Step 1: As a team review the concept of the ladder of inference as just presented, noting the definitions that correspond to each rung on the ladder.

Step 2: Ask each member to place the various statements made during the conversations at the appropriate rungs on the ladder. The following is an example of the ladder of inference that uses statements that might have been made by the Order Cancellation Team (see Chapter Two):

Rung 1: Objective Data and Concrete Evidence ("Order cancellations have doubled over a year ago. There is a backlog entering orders in customer service.")

Rung 2: Interpretation ("Customers are canceling orders because customers are not receiving their new subscriptions.")

Rung 3: Conclusion ("The backlog in entering orders is causing the increase in order cancellations.")

Rung 4: Actions ("We need to reduce the backlog in entering orders right away. That will solve the order cancellation problem.")

Step 3: Members compare how they have placed the statements on the ladder of inference, trying to resolve any areas of disagreement.

Step 4: Beginning with the bottom rung of the ladder, the team seeks to validate whether the evidence at hand justifies ascending to the next rung on the ladder. If not, the team determines what additional information or evidence it needs to obtain to move to the next step on the ladder.

Over the course of its project, the Order Cancellation Team gathered additional evidence that showed that the "rung 2" interpretation was faulty. By sticking to the data rather than jumping to the same conclusions previous teams had when they tackled this problem, the Order Cancellation Team was able to discover a lasting solution to the order cancellation problem.

ACTION STEP 3: EXPLORE DIVERGENT VIEWS

Even when team members raise concerns about where teams are headed and even when warning signs are obvious to everyone involved, they are often ignored or dismissed. In some cases the team members who raised the issues are subtly (or not so subtly) attacked or discredited.

Here are excerpts from the personal logs of three team members commenting on the same meeting:

[Two members] are continually questioning, "What is our purpose? What is our goal?" This is becoming annoying. (Team member 1)

In this session I asked a lot of questions and it seems as though some people thought my questions were holding up the team's progress. (Team member 2)

It seems as though toward the end of this [meeting] there were only a few people participating and they made the final decision that we would stay the course with the project. . . . It was as if we didn't want to stir up any more confusion. (Team member 3)

These logs reveal a very common pattern. A team member (or members) disagrees with the prevailing direction of the team. The person detects resentment from others on the team and, after a few tries, gives up and becomes passive. After such an exchange there are quick and clear winners and losers. Moreover, there has been no opportunity for the team to collectively pursue the merits of alternative approaches.

In contrast, in the radical teams that we studied, a much different form of conversation occurred as teams reflected on their projects. The conversations seemed designed not to produce quick winners and losers but to build mutual understanding by the entire team. These conversations were characterized by team members this way:

- Exploring each other's perspectives as much as, if not more than, trying to convince others that their own views were right

- Presenting objective data and information before drawing conclusions

- Presenting any "conclusions" as hunches to be confirmed or disconfirmed by others rather than hard and fast truths

- Being open to being influenced by others

These characteristics reflect the features of what Peter Senge (1990), borrowing from physicist David Bohm, calls dialogue, which he distinguishes from discussion.

> Bohm points out that the word "discussion" has the same root as percussion and concussion. It suggests something like a "Ping-Pong game where we are hitting the ball back and forth between us." By contrast with discussion, the word "dialogue" comes from the Greek *dialogos*. *Dia* means through. *Logos* means the word, or more broadly the meaning. Bohm suggests that the original meaning of dialogue was the "meaning passing or moving through . . . a free flow of meaning between people, in the sense of a stream that flows between two banks." In dialogue, Bohm contends, a group accesses a larger "pool of common meaning," which cannot be accessed individually [pp. 240–241].

To engage in dialogue, according to Senge, the aim is to maintain a balance between advocacy and inquiry.

APPLICATION EXERCISE 6.3A: THE TALK MODEL

The following is a simple and powerful dialogue technique developed by Karen Watkins and Victoria Marsick and described in their book, *Sculpting the Learning Organization* (1993).

> In dialogue, people should first assert their view of the situation, but they should then inquire about any other possible interpretations of the same situations. . . . We can summarize these steps as the TALK model:

- **T**ell the person with whom you wish to dialogue what you are thinking from the start. Always illustrate your inferences about the situation with examples that you have directly observed or heard that led you to your conclusions.

- **A**sk whether the other party holds the same interpretation of the situation. If not, ask that person for the thinking behind the alternative.

- **L**isten to the other person's response. This may be the most difficult part of the TALK model, because people always interpret what others say by using the meanings they have created for themselves under similar circumstances. Instead of listening carefully to what the other person says, people often jump ahead to their own meanings and judgments. Listening in this model demands that individuals go beyond repeating what was said to stating what they understood, checking to see if this is what was meant, and working to reach consensus on a joint meaning that may differ from where both parties began.

- **K**eep open to the other's views. For talk to be inquiry, both parties must be willing to consider that they do not have all the information they need and that their thinking might not be accurate. People [need to] learn to question the underlying attitude behind their talk, because it is beliefs that drive action [pp. 89–90].

I have had the privilege of working with Watkins and Marsick on several consulting assignments and have observed them using the TALK model. In each case the model was introduced at a point when team members were aggressively advocating their own positions and not really listening to what others were saying, much less inquiring into each other's perspectives. After a quick description and demonstration of the technique, the teams dramatically changed their communication patterns. People started listening to each other. For the first time the teams began to collectively consider divergent points of view that were dismissed or discarded previously.

When it comes to balancing advocacy and inquiry, the struggle for most teams occurs with the inquiry side. To begin with, many of us are not very good listeners. Rick Ross, in *The Fifth Discipline Fieldbook,* offers the following listening guidelines:

1. Stop talking: To others and to yourself. Learn to still the voice within. You can't listen if you are talking.

2. Imagine the other person's viewpoint. Picture yourself in her position, doing her work, facing her problems, using her language, and having her values.

3. Look, act, and be interested. Don't read your mail, doodle, shuffle, or tap papers while others are talking.

4. Observe nonverbal behavior, like body language, to glean meanings beyond what is said to you.

5. Don't interrupt. Sit still past your tolerance level.

6. Listen between the lines, for implicit meanings as well as explicit ones. Consider connotations as well as denotations. Note figures of speech. Instead of accepting a person's remarks as the whole story, look for omissions—things left unsaid or unexplained, which should logically be present. Ask about these.

7. Speak only affirmatively while listening. Resist the temptation to jump in with an evaluative, critical, or disparaging comment at the moment a remark is uttered. Confine yourself to constructive replies until the context has shifted, and criticism can be offered without blame.

8. To ensure understanding, rephrase what the other person has just told you at key points in the conversation. Yes, I know this is the old "active listening" technique, but it works—and how often do you do it?

9. Stop talking. This is a first and last, because all other techniques of listening depend on it. Take a vow of silence once in a while [Senge and Associates, 1994, p. 391].

In most teams members do not ask each other enough questions. They respond quickly without really hearing what other people say. When questions are asked, the questions are not very good. They often steer the conversation in certain directions. They often betray biases. They seldom represent a genuine, open-minded, respectful exploration of points of view that are different from the questioner's own.

The most successful project teams are those that are able to slow things down at critical points, avoid hitting the ball back over the net, and ask each other a series of deep and penetrating questions—questions posed with a true desire to hear and understand the perspective of fellow team members. Here is an exercise designed to get you into the habit of asking these sorts of questions.

APPLICATION EXERCISE 6.3B: A RECIPE FOR MORE AND BETTER QUESTIONS

The next time you are at a project team meeting and you hear an idea you disagree with, try the following recipe for asking more and better questions. Of course, you will not use these guidelines exactly as written all of the time. But they do provide a way of developing some good habits.

Step 1: Take one deep breath. When you first hear a new or different point of view, take a deep breath and avoid "hitting the ball back over the net," even if you strongly disagree. Listen carefully to what other people are saying. Be especially careful to hear the specific data or information that has led others to a conclusion different from yours.

Step 2: Ask three open-ended questions. These are questions that cannot be answered with a simple yes or no. They frequently begin with words such as *how, what, tell me more,* or something similar. Such questions avoid steering the conversation in any direction. They also show that you really want to hear what others have to say. Even very quiet people will tend to open up after a few good open-ended questions. (Avoid questions starting with *why.* Although technically open-ended, they have a tendency to put other people in defensive positions.)

Step 3: Ask three detail questions. Ask at least three questions that try to elicit concrete and objective information. Examples include, How often? How much? Under what circumstances does this usually occur?

Step 4: Ask one provocative question. When appropriate, ask a question designed to challenge the group to think in different ways, such as, What's stopping us from . . . ? What would happen if . . . ?

Step 5: Ask one summary question. Ask a question that invites the group as a whole to summarize and capture its understanding based on the exchange, So where are we now . . . ? What does this mean to the project . . . ? How do other people feel . . . ?

APPLICATION EXERCISE 6.3C: STRIKING A BALANCE

Our studies suggest that most teams tend to engage in much more advocacy than inquiry. However, radical teams in our research studies achieved close to a 50–50 balance. We also found that radical teams had more equal overall participation among team members than the other teams did.

The following team exercise is designed to determine the degree to which a balance exists between advocacy (selling our own ideas) and inquiry (seeking to be influenced by others).

Before a project team meeting, the team designates a team member to serve as the observer for the meeting. This person prepares a grid that looks like the one shown. During the meeting the observer keeps a running tally on the grid of the comments made by each person. (During a two- to three-hour team meeting, I might conduct three observation periods, each about ten minutes long, one toward the beginning of the meeting, one in the middle, and one toward the end.) Each time a person makes an advocacy statement (an assertion in support or defense of a certain position or idea), the observer places a hash mark in the "Advocacy Statements" column. Each time a person makes an inquiry (asks a question, asks for more information, seeks to clarify other people's perspectives), the observer places a hash mark in the "Inquiries" column. At the end of the meeting, the observer calculates the total number and the percentage of the total number of comments made by each person and records the totals in the two far right columns. The observer also calculates the total number and percentage of advocacy statements and inquiries made by the team as a whole and records the totals in the two bottom rows.

The following is an example of how a completed grid might look.

Team Members	Advocacy Statements	Inquiries	Total # per Team Member	Total % per Team Member
Mary	ⅢⅠ ⅢⅠ ⅢⅠ Ⅰ	‖	18	31
Bill	ⅢⅠ Ⅲ	Ⅲ	11	19
Sam	ⅢⅠ ⅢⅠ ⅢⅠ	0	15	25
Mark	‖	‖‖	6	10
Ann	ⅢⅠ	Ⅲ	8	14
Total # for team	47	12	59	N/A
Total % for team	80%	20%	100	100

The observer then presents the completed grid to the team and guides the team in a discussion regarding the following questions:

- What is the overall mixture of advocacy and inquiry for the team as a whole, and do we need to change the balance in the future?

- What is the overall balance of communication among team members, and in the future do we want to change it?

As for the first question, in the example provided, 80 percent of the comments were advocacy statements, and 20 percent were inquiries. This result suggests that the team needs to reduce the frequency of advocacy statements and increase the number of inquiries if it wants to establish a balance between advocacy and inquiry.

Regarding the communication balance, in the team discussion charted earlier, there were five team members. If communication were totally balanced, each person would have received 20 percent of the hash marks. In the example, two members, Mary and Sam, had more than the 20 percent average, together making 56 percent of the team's comments. Two members, Mark and Ann, made significantly fewer comments than the 20 percent average. In future meetings, the team may decide that it should strike more of an overall balance of participation, with Mark and Ann increasing their contributions and Mary and Sam decreasing theirs.

Based on this discussion, the team determines whatever changes in communication patterns it wants to make in future meetings. It is suggested that the team repeat this exercise at several different meetings over the course of the project, with other team members serving as observers.

ACTION STEP 4: USE BREAKDOWNS TO PRODUCE BREAKTHROUGHS

From time to time almost all teams experience episodes characterized by frustration, anger, and personal conflict among team members. Most teams have a very low tolerance for such apparent breakdowns in effective teamwork. One of the most surprising findings from our studies was that *periods of intense frustration, anger, and conflict often immediately precede the reframing of projects.*

In other words breakdowns were often necessary for breakthroughs to occur. This finding suggests that teams need to adopt a whole new mind-set when it comes to handling conflict and other impasses. These should be seen, not as breakdowns in team process but as natural and inevitable components of the learning process. Teams need to become much more comfortable with being uncomfortable. This requires a new way to look at conflict.

The following is a typical example of how conflict is often handled in project teams.

The Failed Restructuring Team

In response to declining enrollment and aggressive competition from other academic institutions, a mid-sized college restructured itself into market-focused business units. Traditional academic departments were disbanded, and several autonomous business units were established, each structured around a specific market segment (such as students of traditional age, returning students, and business and industry). Six months after the restructuring, the school was in turmoil. High levels of personal conflict existed among administration and faculty in the new business units. Several faculty members threatened to resign, feeling that this new structure was compromising academic standards.

A project team was formed to see what could be done to salvage the restructuring initiative. During the first meeting the team decided to put together a questionnaire to solicit the opinions of faculty and staff regarding the restructuring. Several team members felt that the questions should focus on the staff development needed to help people assume their new roles in the restructured organization. Although the majority of team members felt comfortable with this idea (one member wrote, "I felt as though we were all on the same page"), at least one member, Chris, felt that the team needed to take a broader look at the issues. After the first meeting, Chris wrote in her log, "I feel as if we are jumping to a solution." However, she did not express this concern in the meeting.

By the third meeting a rough draft of the questionnaire had been developed, with most of the questions related to staff development needs. Chris's frustration level was mounting. She wrote in her log:

> I am still confused. How did we get to this point? Why are we focusing on staff development? How do we know that this is the problem? I feel bad because I didn't raise my concerns, and I am still uncomfortable with this direction.

However, rather than directly present her concerns about the project, Chris suggested several revisions to the survey questionnaire, inserting questions that sought staff input on a wide range of different issues, including the effectiveness of the new structure, staff input in decision making, and the overall academic quality of the institution. Chris left the meeting believing that the questions would be incorporated into the final survey. David, another team member, volunteered to produce a final draft of the questionnaire and fax it to the others for final review. However, David had no intention of making the changes Chris had suggested.

> I grew more weary with Chris's lack of understanding of what we were accomplishing. I felt the task that we established . . . was being met. So I just decided to produce the final draft myself so as to not stir up any more confusion.

When Chris received the fax and discovered that her proposed questions were not included, she was furious:

> After I received the fax, I realized that my questions were changed, losing their original meaning and purpose. I felt ignored. I felt frustrated. At the next session, I didn't talk. When I was asked to express my opinion, I said something irrelevant and unimportant, hiding my real thoughts and feelings. Again I received the impression that everybody was working in different directions without knowing what we were doing and what we were trying to create.

Six weeks later the team met to review the survey results. The team was disappointed in the results. There was little interest in staff development, and there were rather superficial responses to the open-ended questions. About an hour into the meeting, Chris decided she couldn't take it much longer. Chris later wrote in her log, "I decided I had had enough. I told the team what I really felt."

Chris interrupted the discussion of the survey results, her soft voice trembling with emotion as she began to speak:

> This whole thing is driving me crazy. I wake up at night thinking about this project. I am an introvert, so it is hard for me to speak up. I am not sure where we are headed. I think we missed the boat. It's still foggy to me why people need training. I feel we're putting it on the staff. That they were the problem. Maybe it's me, but I'd like to take a look at how we got to this point.

Mary, a director of one the new business units, cut Chris off in mid-sentence, responding:

> We're to blame. We took people who have no background or skill in working in teams. They are great teachers. But they've never had to work together to solve problems. We need to provide them with the help needed to work effectively together. We need team building. There's no trust.

Chris, feeling that her ideas were being dismissed, responded angrily, her voice rising in volume for the first time:

> I never really understood why we went ahead with the restructuring so fast. This was rammed down our throats by people who care more about building empires and careers than educating students. We're no longer in the education business; we're just in business. I . . .

At that point, several other team members jumped in trying to calm things down. After some more discussion, the team agreed to recommend a series of team-building retreats for each of the business units. Several members knew consultants who did team-building programs. It was agreed that at the next meeting the group would identify a small group of consultants to be interviewed and put together an outline for a team-building retreat.

This story is typical in several ways:

- Chris kept her concerns to herself for most of the project, trying to avoid conflict with other members of the team.
- She voiced her concerns only after her own frustration levels had risen to a peak.
- The team felt uncomfortable with the situation and quickly changed the subject.

Most significant, in an episode like the one just described an opportunity for learning was lost. It is moments such as these, when conflict and tension are at their highest levels, that teams are most apt to question original assumptions and to get previously unstated perspectives on the table. It is possible that the restructuring had, as some faculty had suspected, diminished academic standards. It is possible that the new structure, while giving the illusion of shared governance, did not allow for any real, meaningful input of staff in decision making. However, these possibilities were never explored by the team.

In contrast to what occurred in this example, it is important that teams use episodes of frustration and conflict as opportunities for learning. To do so, teams need to stop and take a look at what is going on and explore the implications for their projects. The focus of these examinations should not be limited to the individuals who are exhibiting signs of frustration, anger, and conflict. Instead, teams as a whole should objectively examine such episodes as a means of deriving important project insights.

For example, imagine that rather than quickly changing the subject, members of the Failed Restructuring Team had stopped and reflected on what was happening in the meeting. Here is an exercise that a project team might use at such a point:

APPLICATION EXERCISE 6.4: REFLECTING ON ROADBLOCKS AND BREAKDOWNS

Use the following steps to explore roadblocks and breakdowns as a means of producing project breakthroughs.

Step 1: The team agrees to take a time out from discussing the project to explore what is causing the team to get stuck. To get things started, someone might say: "I have a feeling we are getting hung up here as a team, and it might be useful to take a look at what is going on."

Step 2: Ask team members to spend five to ten minutes reflecting on what has just occurred in the meeting, thinking about their responses to the following questions:

• What exactly happened?

• What were you feeling and thinking at the time?

Step 3: Ask each member of the group to describe specifically what he or she observed and was feeling at the time.

Example: "I noticed that Chris had not talked yet during the meeting. And when she was asked a question, she said something that seemed unrelated to what was being asked. I felt that she was upset about something, but I didn't understand why."

As people are expressing their points of view, other team members agree to follow these guidelines:

- Do not interrupt, except to ask clarification questions.
- Do not comment, either supporting or disagreeing with what the person said.

Step 4: One member from the team volunteers to summarize the various perspectives that have just been presented in an objective statement:

Example: "It seems as if a few of us have had some strong reservations about the approach we've been taking and that the team has not seemed to want to explore these ideas. Others feel confident that we are on the right track and are frustrated that we are not further along with the project."

Other team members then comment regarding the degree to which this statement accurately reflects the different perspectives of the team members. Team members should not state whether they agree or disagree with what the statement says, only whether it accurately captures the varying perspectives of team members. In addition, there should be no attempt to discuss possible solutions or next steps.

Step 5: Team members agree to put aside these perspectives for a period of time and, as a team, try to engage in a joint learning process to discover the best way to approach the project. Someone might pose questions similar to these: "How can we move together as a whole team? How might we verify that our present approach is on target or whether we should be taking a different approach?"

Step 6: The team then determines a series of concrete action steps that can be taken before the team's next meeting to obtain information needed to move the team forward.

Step 7: Finally, the team explores what can be learned from what occurred in the meeting that might help the team work more effectively in the future.

Example: Chris might say, "I realize that I need to come out and directly say that I do not agree with a decision and not just sit there and keep things bottled up."

Example: Another team member might say, "I knew that Chris did not agree with what we were doing, but I pushed us to go ahead anyway. In the future, I think we should stop and make sure everyone is on board before we proceed."

ACTION STEP 5: CAPTURE LESSONS LEARNED FROM CYCLE TO CYCLE

Capturing lessons learned at the end of projects is becoming more and more prevalent. However, it is still fairly rare that teams stop and identify what has been learned as projects progress. Radical teams seek to collectively and explicitly capture what has been learned as a result of one cycle before moving to the next. They treat "learnings" as tangible team products, just as important as other deliverables produced by teams such as market studies, business case analyses, and proposals.

In listening to the audiotapes of dozens of teams, our research group discovered a very interesting phenomenon: teams would often capture the learnings in short catchphrases or metaphors. Here are some examples:

- "The ship has no rudder."
- "We are shooting blanks out there."
- "We don't have our act together."
- "It's a lot bigger than we thought it was."

To the teams, these catchphrases embodied powerful new insights. In most cases they represented newly discovered understandings that the issues they were struggling with in their projects were merely manifestations of much deeper issues—issues that were often both systemic (affecting the organization as a whole) and strategic (addressing their firms' competitive positioning in the marketplace). Only by dealing with these deeper issues would the project be successfully completed. For example, the expression "We are shooting blanks out there" captured the Order Cancellation Team's recognition that CPR's product line was obsolete.

It was interesting to watch these catchphrases first emerge and then take hold in their teams. One team member would use the phrase almost in passing. The conversation might continue for several minutes, and then another team member would use the same phrase, and then in another few minutes, another person. The phrases seemed to resonate with special meaning for the teams. In almost every meeting from then on, the phrase would be liberally sprinkled into team discussions and spoken with a deference to the deep truths it embodied.

The power of these catchphrases stems from the fact that they served as simple shorthand to refer to complex understandings that the teams achieved over the course of their projects. The capturing of these learnings is the core of the radical teamwork process of this book. Everything else is designed either to establish the conditions needed to produce these learnings or to help teams maximize the impact of these learnings on the organization.

The following two application exercises provide structured methods that teams can use to help identify lessons learned.

APPLICATION EXERCISE 6.5A: CAPTURING LESSONS LEARNED

Use the following steps to capture lessons learned at key points in your project.

Step 1: After your team has reviewed the new information that has been acquired since the last time it met, ask team members to stop and engage in five to ten minutes of silent, personal reflection regarding what has been learned so far, thinking about the following questions:

- What do we know now that we didn't know earlier?

- Have there been any surprises or new insights? If so, what are they?

- To what degree have previous assumptions been supported or refuted by what we have learned so far?

- How do you feel about the project at this point? How do you feel about the effectiveness of the team at this point?

- What ideas or thoughts about the project do you have that you have not yet shared with the team?

Step 2: After five to ten minutes of silent reflection, ask each team member to summarize his or her responses to these questions. This should not be a group discussion. Each person should express his or her perspectives without interruption or comment from others. The only interruption should be for clarification questions, such as "What did you mean when you said . . . ?" Within reason, people should be allowed to talk as long as they want to.

Step 3: After everyone has had a chance to talk, the team as a whole identifies the common themes they heard in individual comments.

Step 4: The whole team then reaches agreement on the key learnings that have occurred and explores their implications for the project.

APPLICATION EXERCISE 6.5B:
THE ASSUMPTION-LEARNING GRID

Follow these steps to determine whether your original assumptions are supported or refuted by what your team has learned.

Step 1: Ask someone to draw a two-column grid like the following on a flip chart:

Column 1 Previous Assumptions (What We Thought Was True)	Column 2 What We've Learned

Step 2: In Column 1 the team lists as many as possible of the original assumptions the team held about the project.

Step 3: After all assumptions have been recorded, team members go back and identify what has been learned to date about each assumption, writing what has been learned in the second column. Team members share the concrete data and objective information on which they are basing their conclusions. Before writing anything in the second column, there should be consensus from all team members regarding each item. The Assumption-Learning Grid might look like this:

Column 1 Previous Assumptions (What We Thought Was True)	Column 2 What We've Learned
The project's scope is too big. We are being asked to make recommendations on ten different products. Realistically, we should only have to deal with one or two product lines.	The project is more realistic than we thought. Any decision is likely to affect many different products. A few key factors will probably drive all products.

Column 1 Previous Assumptions (What We Thought Was True)	Column 2 What We've Learned
Management is not really committed to doing something. Several teams have worked on this project before. Senior managers weren't willing to invest the money or take the risks required. Like the previous teams, our recommendations will likely not be implemented.	The project has very high corporate support. The CEO is putting pressure to get this issue resolved. This product line is making only 50% of the contribution of the corporate average. There is a recognition that significant financial and market resources may be required.
As a team, we do not have the skills needed to do the job.	The problem is not a technical problem. It's a marketing and management issue. Technical resources are available to us.

ACTION STEP 6: REFRAME THE PROJECT

At the beginning of each new learning cycle, it is important that project teams synthesize what has been learned so far, deepen their understandings of their projects, and if necessary, reframe their projects as a result. Here are some examples of reframing drawn from projects described earlier in this book:

• For the Order Cancellation Project, it was only when the problem was redefined as a strategic marketing issue that the team was able to generate true solutions to the order cancellation problem.

• For the Cochlear Implant Project, very early in the project the team restricted itself to producing single-channel devices designed for the severely hearing impaired. It took over fifteen years for the project to be reframed to include both multichannel and single-channel devices and cover the mildly impaired and moderately impaired as well as the severely impaired. The failure to redefine the project earlier cost the company millions of dollars.

• For the Failed Restructuring Project, the team quickly defined the project as providing staff development needed to make the restructuring work. After considerable struggle among team members, the team eventually reframed its project to include a much wider set of issues that had the potential to affect the success of the restructuring, including participation in decision making, academic standards, and recognition and rewards.

An obvious similarity exists among the ways these projects were eventually redefined. All three projects were initially defined in ways that contained embedded solutions. The redefined projects defined the root problem or task, discarding the assumptions made previously.

Another similarity exists in the ways these projects were reframed. The reframing occurred not during a single learning cycle but over the course of multiple learning cycles. There appear to be two reasons why reframing requires multiple learning cycles. First, after a single cycle it might be possible to see that the project framing is problematic. This was the case with the Order Cancellation Team. After the very first cycle, the team saw that the real issue was not the order cancellation process in customer service. However, it took several more cycles for the project to become fully reframed, with the team's collective realization that "we are shooting blanks out there." And second, reframing needs to be a collective team act. The only way to tell that collective reframing has occurred is to look at the actions that come out of the team meetings. If the actions look much like previous actions, no collective reframing has occurred. If actions look much different, then it is clear that reframing has happened. In most of the teams we studied, one or more members advocated the reframing of projects much earlier than did the teams as a whole. Yet the teams continued down the same paths. For example, with the Failed Restructuring Team it took multiple cycles to occur, with increasing levels of frustration and conflict, for the team as a whole to finally reframe the project.

When reframing their projects, team members need to ask themselves the same basic questions they asked at the beginning:

- What is the purpose of our project?
- What goals or outcomes are we trying to achieve?
- What end deliverables do we need to produce?
- What resources (financial, human resources, among others) are available to the team?
- Do we have the right people on the team?
- Who are key stakeholders and what are their relationships to the project?
- What limitations exist?
- What is the expected time line for the project?

As part of the reframing process, it may be necessary to alter team charters or other written documents to reflect the proposed changes. Team members may need to have conversations with key project stakeholders, such as project sponsors, to clarify any project changes. They may need to obtain approvals for any proposed extensions of time lines, additional project expenditures, or changes in team membership.

The following exercise helps teams reframe their projects, based on what they have learned as a result of previous learning cycles.

APPLICATION EXERCISE 6.6: PROJECT REFRAMING GRID

This exercise is best completed just after your team has achieved some significant learnings that have the potential to change the way your team is defining its project.

Step 1: A grid like the following should be drawn on a flip chart.

	Column 1 Original Project Definition	Column 2 Proposed Changes to Project Definition
Purpose of project		
Desired goals or outcomes		
End deliverables		
Resources		
Time line		

Step 2: For each category on the side of the grid, the team should go through the following two-step process:

In Column 1 describe the way that the project was originally framed.

In Column 2 identify how the project should be reframed as a result of what has been learned.

Step 3: Continue the same process for each category on the grid.

Step 4: After the entire grid is complete, the team identifies the specific action steps that need to be taken as a result of the project reframing. Here are some key questions the team might ask:

- Do any written documents need to be changed or completed to reflect the proposed changes?
- Do conversations need to occur with any key project stakeholders, such as the project sponsor?
- Do any other approvals need to be obtained (such as extensions of time lines or additional project expenditures)?
- Does the project team make-up still make sense, or should there be some changes to the make-up of the team?

The following presents a hypothetical example of what a reframing grid might have looked like for the Cochlear Implant Project if, after a few learning cycles, the project team was able to reframe its project successfully.

	Column 1 Original Project Definition	Column 2 Proposed Changes to Project Definition
Purpose of project	Develop a single-channel cochlear implant for the severely hearing disabled.	Develop a cochlear implant device to serve the mild-to-moderately hearing disabled.
Desired goals or outcomes	Be first to market with a device.	Capture dominant market share.
End deliverables	Consider safety above all else. Meet needs of severely disabled.	Meet FDA requirements; meet the needs of targeted market segments better than competitive products and have a competitive edge with respect to quality, cost, and convenience.
Resources	Financial resources are unlimited.	Annual expenditures not to exceed 10% of projected after-tax profits, annualized over the first five years after project launch.

	Column 1 Original Project Definition	Column 2 Proposed Changes to Project Definition
Time line	Product will be launched within five years.	Team should look for opportunities for short-term product launches and then phase in existing projects.

As shown by the grid, the reframed project has several key differences from the original. The team is no longer assuming that single-channel devices are the way to go; however, the team is not yet ruling out single-channel devices. It is looking at a potentially broader market and customer base than just the severely hearing impaired market. It is considering a much wider set of success criteria for the project, with safety being only one of several key product features needed for success. It is recognizing that there are realistic financial limits to what the corporation should invest in the project, and these limits are specified for the first time. It is also avoiding committing to arbitrary time lines for a product launch.

This chapter presented a series of action steps designed to enhance the depth of learning:

Action Step 1: Make it safe.

Action Step 2: Detect early warning signs.

Action Step 3: Explore divergent views.

Action Step 4: Exploit breakdowns to produce breakthroughs.

Action Step 5: Capture lessons learned from cycle to cycle.

Action Step 6: Reframe projects to reflect deepening understandings.

The next chapter presents five action steps for increasing the breadth of learning.

chapter
SEVEN

Impact
*Action Steps to Increase
the Breadth of Team Learning*

They changed the whole company.

A project champion describing one of the radical teams featured in this book

Previous chapters presented action steps related to speed and depth. Speed reflects the degree to which projects are approached as a learning process; radical teams accelerate their learning by engaging in rapid fire cycles of discovery. Depth relates to the quality of learning that occurs during projects; radical teams deepen their understandings of their projects as they progress, seeking to produce project breakthroughs.

This chapter covers the third dimension—breadth. Breadth is concerned with the degree to which the scope of a project is widened over time; radical teams are able to achieve broad and pervasive impact on the organization as whole systems, often affecting issues critical to the strategic success of the enterprise. In some cases organizations are transformed, maybe for years and years to come, because of the work of individual project teams.

147

Radical teams approach their projects with a different mind-set than do most other teams. Most teams seek to keep their projects defined within prescribed boundaries. Radical teams understand that their projects are embedded within systemic and strategic contexts. They perceive themselves as acting as agents for entire organizations. They understand that their assumptions are at some level reflections of the collective assumptions of their firms.

The following action steps are based on observations of radical teams:

Action Step 1: Uncover connections.

Action Step 2: Reach out to influence others.

Action Step 3: Learn from past projects.

Action Step 4: Go against the organizational grain.

Action Step 5: Make things happen elsewhere.

The Production Scheduling Team

The company designs and manufactures point-of-sale marketing materials for a segment of the home furnishings business. There has been an industry shake-out over recent years. Only a few players are left. Competition for their business is getting tougher and tougher. As a result the company relies on only a handful of very large customers for the bulk of its business. These customers are putting increasing pressure on the company for both quicker turnaround and reduced prices.

The company is being caught in a cost squeeze. It built its reputation on doing whatever it takes to meet customer demands. Located in the middle of a large urban center, it can bring in hundreds of temporary workers with just a few days notice. Unlike its major competitors, the company has also built up the capability to do almost all parts of jobs in-house, allowing it to be more flexible and responsive. However, the ability to turn around large, complex jobs faster than anybody else has its downsides: higher overhead and direct labor costs. Now with intensifying demands to reduce prices more and more while meeting even more aggressive time lines, the company's profitability has eroded. The company even lost money on a few recent jobs.

One way the company decided to tackle the problem was to form a Production Scheduling Team. Management felt that an improved production scheduling process would likely reduce both costs and turnaround time. Team members included customer service staff, production planners, production coordinators, and production managers.

Cycle 1: Before delving into the production scheduling process, the team decided to gain a better understanding of the overall production process. Each person understood part of the picture, but no one knew how everything fit together. Team members scheduled a walk-through of the building, tracing what happens to a job from the time an order is placed until products are shipped out the door. At each step in the process they discussed roadblocks and problems affecting cost and turnaround time.

Cycle 2: After the production tour, members expressed differing views regarding the scope of the team's project. Some people felt it should be limited to developing better production schedules. Others felt that the ultimate aim was to reduce production costs and turnaround time and that many issues were involved other than just production scheduling.

The team decided to take a few minutes and explore what these other factors might be. Someone got up and wrote in the middle of the white board at the front of the room the following question: How might we reduce both production costs and turnaround time? People started brainstorming ideas, including the following:

- Reducing labor costs through less overtime, decreased use of temporary workers, and increased productivity.
- Keeping to production schedules, including starting jobs as scheduled and minimizing any changes to production schedules (either by the customer or by the company). Customers generally supply the raw material needed to do jobs; however, sometimes the materials do not arrive on time and delay the start of production. Yet in most cases customers still expect the company to meet the deadline for final shipment.
- Decreasing overhead by increasing the use of equipment.
- Avoiding rework.
- Changing the company policy that it will do whatever it takes to meet the customer's requirements for delivery.

As these ideas were thrown out, they were diagrammed on a white board as shown in Figure 7.1.

Figure 7.1
Domain Map for Production Scheduling Project

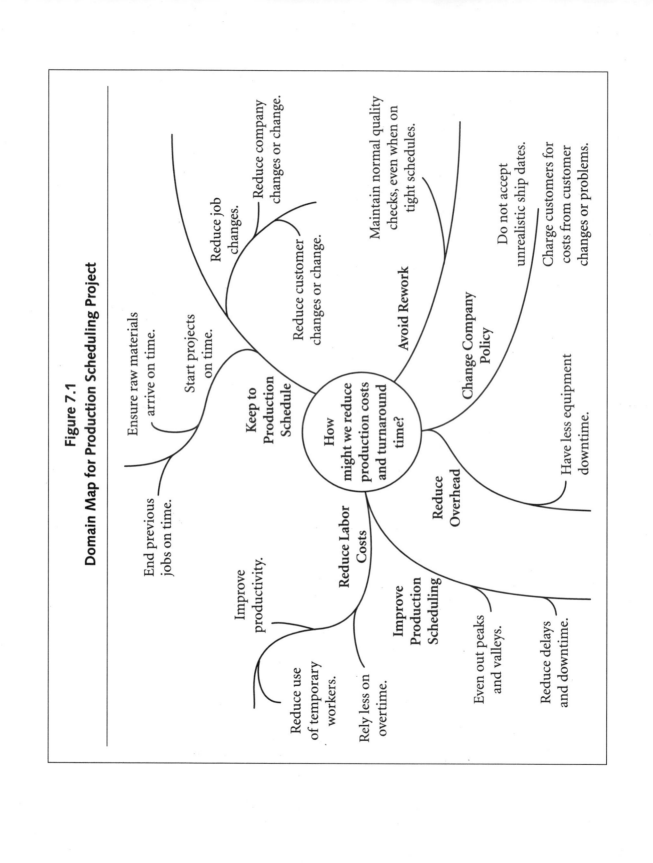

The team decided to investigate certain items diagrammed on the white board for which more information was needed.

Cycle 3: After gathering more information, the team took another look at the diagram and examined the relative impact of each item on the goal of reducing both costs and turnaround time. Almost everything listed would do one or the other. Only a few would seem to do both at the same time. One was the issue of customer-supplied raw materials. If customers ensured that raw materials were delivered to the company on time, both costs and production turnaround time would likely decrease. In addition, the team was surprised by the severity of the problem: at least 50 percent of the time, customer-supplied materials were coming in later than needed to start production. One member, who was relatively new to the company, commented, "You really have a crazy system here. How can you plan production when you can't count on materials getting here as scheduled?"

Several members of the team argued that it was useless to develop a production scheduling process without addressing this underlying problem. Other people felt that this was outside the scope of the project. The team agreed to meet with the company's executive committee (the company's president and three executive vice presidents) to obtain clarification on the scope of the project. All work on the project was halted until a meeting could be scheduled.

To prepare for the executive committee meeting, the team developed the following questions:

- Is it our job to develop a production scheduling process or to reduce costs and turnaround time?
- Are we supposed to do a major overhaul or just a fix-it job?
- Are we overstepping our bounds if we suggest that the whole system needs to be looked at?

The Production Scheduling Team and the executive committee met for about an hour. Throughout the entire meeting, members of the executive committee did not express any opinions. They just asked the team to explain what it had discovered so far and why the team was recommending broadening the scope of the project. After the team left, the executive committee had a lengthy discussion, finally agreeing that the team should broaden the scope of its project.

Cycle 4: The team continued to investigate the problem, getting more detailed information and using the diagram as a guide. It invited the company's top outside sales representative to join the team to help look at customer-related issues.

Cycle 5: The team updated the diagram, based on the new information it had gathered. It was now able to identify some specific underlying factors influencing those listed earlier. For example, the problem with customer-supplied raw materials seemed related to customers moving to just-in-time inventory systems over recent years. Because customers were operating with tighter and tighter inventories, they were finding it harder to supply raw materials as promised.

Looking at the diagram, someone asked, "How are all of these items interrelated? If we were to fix one of these items, would that also fix other problems at all?" So the team began drawing lines from item to item on the diagram, showing how each item was related to the next. Two issues stood out as most central: (1) the degree to which customer-supplied raw materials are delivered on time and (2) the company policy that it will absorb the increased costs resulting from customers not meeting their commitments to ship raw materials on time. If these two issues were resolved, most of the other items seemed to present relatively quick fixes.

The team debated whether it would be backed up by senior management if it developed recommendations focused on these issues. As someone said, "This represents a major shift in our company philosophy. The first time we go to tell a customer that we're going to raise the price because they had not gotten the raw materials here on time, senior management will overrule us." The team decided to ask for another meeting with the executive committee to present its analysis and directly ask whether it should continue down this path.

Cycle 6: This time the meeting with the executive committee did not appear to go very smoothly. The members of the executive committee openly disagreed with each other as to what to do. The meeting concluded without the team receiving any final word on continuing with the project. About a week and several heated executive committee meetings later, the committee gave the team the go-ahead to develop a set of detailed recommendations regarding these two issues. The team was told it should also work with the salesforce and talk to several top customers and gauge their support for any recommendations.

Cycle 7: The team had meetings with several of its top customers. Across the board, customers understood the company's need to assess a surcharge if raw materials did not arrive as scheduled. During these discussions several customers brought up the possibility of linking the two firms' computer systems using electronic data interchange (EDI). Among other things, EDI would allow the company to have real-time information about the status of customer-supplied raw materials, including how much is in stock, when raw materials are scheduled to be shipped, and if they had actually been shipped. One customer invited the company to join an EDI pilot program being conducted with several key vendors over the next six months.

About a month later, the team presented a proposal to the executive committee. The plan included the proposed EDI pilot program, followed by full implementation with other customers over the next two years. An EDI team would be formed, and the Production Scheduling Team would continue its work in parallel, piloting a production scheduling process at the same time. In addition, the team proposed a procedure through which all new jobs would require that customers sign a commitment to deliver raw materials on time or be subject to late penalties.

Three years later the results look very positive. Unit production costs are down by one-third. Production cycle time has been reduced by 20 percent. The implementation of EDI took longer than expected. However, in the process of working on the EDI project the company started receiving better information about customer-supplied inventory than it had ever received before. As a result the problem of late shipments was significantly reduced within just a few months. Most important, the establishment of EDI sparked the creation of a "strategic partnership" program through which the company has been designated as the first choice supplier by three customers. Through this program the company is now receiving 80 percent of the available business from these partnership customers.

The Production Scheduling Team was successful because it engaged in what Peter Senge (1990), in *The Fifth Discipline,* calls systems thinking. Organizations are bound, Senge explains, "by invisible fabrics of interrelated actions, which often take years to fully play out their effects upon each other. Since we are part of that lacework ourselves, it's doubly hard to see the whole pattern of change. Instead, we tend to focus on snapshots of isolated parts of the system, and wonder why our deepest problems never seem to get solved" (p. 7). Systems thinking gives us the ability to see through complex situations and detect "the underlying structures generating change" (p. 128). As a result teams are able to distinguish between low-payoff, quick fixes and high pay-off, enduring solutions.

That is clearly what the Production Scheduling Team did. The team unraveled complex interrelationships that were having unintended consequences. Ironically, the company's attempt to do whatever it took to satisfy the customer was producing the opposite effect: the company could not satisfy customers' demands for lower costs and quicker turnaround.

Systems thinking sometimes sounds like an esoteric, conceptual exercise. In reality it is anything but. As shown by the Production Scheduling Team, systems thinking is a full contact sport. It is not enough that the team uncovered these complex interrelationships. It had to get other stakeholders—senior management, the salesforce, and customers—to come to the same realization. To do so, the team had to "work the system." It refused to be limited by predetermined project boundaries. It reached out and involved key stakeholders in finding a solution. It was aggressive and assertive in making things happen. Yet it was also street-wise in managing the politics of the situation.

Next I describe a series of action steps that radical teams take to maximize the breadth of impact they have on their organizations.

ACTION STEP 1: UNCOVER CONNECTIONS

Radical teams search out potentially relevant factors. They do not just wait for issues to appear. From the beginning of their projects, they embrace a systems perspective, recognizing that any specific problems being addressed are likely being influenced by a range of other issues that, at least initially, might seem unrelated, such as the following:

- Marketplace issues, including changes in customer needs and expectations, competitive moves, industry trends, and economic and demographic shifts

- Technology issues, including advances in information processing, production methods, and communications

- Supply chain issues, including relationships with vendors and distributors

- Functional issues in the areas of finance, research and development, sales and marketing, and production

- Process issues, including how the organization processes orders, services customers, and resolves quality problems
- Human resource issues, including staffing levels, skills and competencies, performance management, and rewards and recognition
- Organizational issues, including strategic business goals and plans, company cultures, organizational structures, and relationships within and between business units

Teams need to exhibit high levels of curiosity, gathering information and exploring any potential variables that might be related to their projects.

It is often useful for teams to visually represent the system they are attempting to influence. The Production Scheduling Team used a technique often referred to as a domain map or mind map (Pacanowsky, 1995; Wycloff, 1991), as shown in Figure 7.1. This method is different from traditional brainstorming techniques because it seeks to visually portray the complex interrelationships that exist rather than just create an itemized list. The following are guidelines for mapping a problem or task using the domain map or mind-map process.

APPLICATION EXERCISE 7.1A: CREATING A DOMAIN MAP

Use the following steps to identify potential forces and factors affecting your team's project.

Step 1: Draw a circle in the middle of a flip chart page or white board, containing a question such as, What are the major factors and forces potentially affecting our project?

Step 2: As members suggest various items to be listed, draw each one as a branch coming off the central circle. Each branch then in turn can have multiple limbs, providing more specific breakdowns of each issue.

Step 3: After the team finishes listing all items that it feels are relevant, ask members to identify which issues it needs to investigate further by gathering more information and reporting back to the team at subsequent meetings. Of special interest to the team is finding how the various factors on the map are related to each other. For example, do certain items seem to be causal factors that appear to influence one or more other items on the map?

Step 4: Later on in the project, after the team has investigated the items on the map, it then returns to the map and discusses the interrelationships among the various items. This can be done by drawing lines connecting two interrelated factors. Or when possible, arrows can be drawn pointing from one factor to another factor, suggesting how they might be influencing each other.

Step 5: Looking at the map as a whole, the team then identifies the small group of factors that seem to be most important. For example, if lines or arrows are drawn from one item to six others, it is likely that the first item is one that represents a high-leverage opportunity for solutions. The team can then focus its remaining efforts on exploring how these high-leverage issues could be handled.

As shown by the Production Scheduling Team in Figure 7.1, domain maps are powerful because they have the potential to both expand the range of issues examined by teams and to help the team focus its efforts on the most critical factors.

Trace the Narrow Back to the Broad

Not all factors are of the same scope. Some are comparatively narrow; others are broad and encompassing. Figure 7.2 shows how issues facing project teams can be placed on a narrow-to-broad continuum. Examples are drawn from the story of the Order Cancellation Team (see Chapter Two).

• *Within Function or Business Unit.* These factors are limited to the operations of specific functions or business units. *Example:* There is an order entry backlog in the customer service department.

Figure 7.2
The Narrow-to-Broad Continuum

Within Function or Unit	Across Function or Unit	Whole Organization	Organization or Environment	External Environment

Narrow ————————————————————————→ Broad

- *Across Function or Business Unit.* These issues pertain to the interrelationships between functions or business units. *Example:* The sales department is rebooking orders without asking customers, which is causing increased order cancellations in the customer service department.

- *Whole Organization.* These issues pertain to the overall operations of the company. *Example:* The company was purchased by a large, diversified corporation, which is imposing standards for company performance, including sales, profitability, and market share.

- *Organization or Environment.* These issues deal with the organization's plans and strategies related to business conditions. *Example:* As a company our business strategy is to focus on large corporations and offer them accurate and timely summaries of industry changes on a monthly and quarterly subscription basis.

- *External Environment.* These issues relate to business conditions and operate independently of organizations. *Example:* New competitors have entered the market offering on-line electronic products via the Internet.

Over the course of projects, teams need to move along the continuum, from narrow to broad, as needed, to produce successful project outcomes. Do all projects need to end up at the far right of the continuum? They do not. Organizations still face many issues that are limited to specific functional areas or business issues. However, with the fast-changing external environments, it is becoming increasingly the case that narrowly defined, internal issues turn out to be symptomatic of broad forces in the marketplace. Moreover, it is unlikely that organizations would dedicate the resources and time needed to deploy cross-functional project teams if the issues were narrow in scope.

APPLICATION EXERCISE 7.1B: USING THE NARROW-TO-BROAD CONTINUUM

At key points in the project, your team can use the continuum presented in Figure 7.2 to identify the current scope of your project and determine if its scope needs to be broadened.

Step 1: Draw a continuum such as the one presented in Figure 7.2 on a flip chart or white board visible to the whole team.

Step 2: Ask team members to think about how the team has been approaching the project so far. They should consider the way the project was originally defined, the types of information gathered, and recent team discussions regarding potential issues that might be relevant to the project.

Step 3: Ask team members to share their individual perceptions regarding the scope of the project.

Step 4: The team then reaches overall agreement on the current scope of the project, placing an "X" at the spot on the continuum that is at the point farthest to the right that represents how the team has been approaching the project so far.

Step 5: The team should then discuss how they might need to further broaden the scope of the project. To do so, the team should locate the spot on the continuum that is to the immediate right of where the "X" was placed. For example:

- If the "X" was placed at "Within Function or Business Unit," the team should ask whether there are any "Across Function or Business Unit" issues that should be explored.

- If the "X" was placed at "Across Function or Business Unit," the team should ask whether there are any "Whole Organization" issues that should be explored.

- If the "X" was placed at "Whole Organization," the team should ask if there are any "Organization or Environment" issues that need to be explored.

- If the "X" was placed at "Organization or Environment," the team should ask if there are any "External Environmental" issues that need to be explored.

Step 6: The team should put together an action plan of steps that can be quickly taken to further investigate the issues identified.

Understand Complex Cause-Effect Relationships

One of the most difficult tasks of project teams is to reach shared understandings regarding the complex interrelationships among various factors influencing their projects. There are several reasons why this is so hard to do. First, it is inherently difficult for groups of people to jointly explore the complexities and subtleties of cause-and-effect relationships. It takes a lot of time for people to make sure they all understand things the same way. Second, the evidence supporting cause-and-effect relationships might be pretty sketchy. It might take teams quite some effort to verify that these relationships in fact exist. Finally, lengthy delays often exist between causes and their effects. For example, it might take years for broad forces (such as changes in the external environment) to have an impact on narrow factors inside organizations (such as operational problems being experienced by specific departments).

Teams need to take the time and make the effort to explore the relationships among the many variables that might be influencing their projects. As noted earlier, teams need some visual representation to illustrate the connections they are seeing among a broad range of factors in the organizations. The domain map as just presented is useful, especially at early stages of projects, because it serves to highlight a wide range of different factors and begins exploring their interrelationships.

Peter Senge (1990) offers another tool: system archetypes.[1] This approach provides templates of several classic patterns of cause-effect relationships that emerge in organizations over time. For example, one archetype is called Fixes That Fail. This pattern shows how a solution that has positive short-term results often has unintended consequences and makes the problem worse in the long term. Another is called Shifting the Burden, in which organizations that are struggling with a problem turn to the outside for help, which makes them less able to solve problems in the future and more dependent on outside help. After becoming acquainted with these archetypes, teams can then look at their own projects and see if any of these patterns apply. I have found systems archetypes especially useful toward the middle of projects, after teams have identified a range of interrelated factors and are now seeking to understand how they interrelate.

Another approach is the reverse flow chart. Teams find this technique most helpful at later stages of projects, when they need to explain to others complex sets of cause-and-effect relationships. The reverse flow chart is a great way to tell a story.

APPLICATION EXERCISE 7.1C: REVERSE FLOW CHART

Your team can use basic flow-charting methods to illustrate the relationships among various issues affecting your projects. In most cases only a few basic flow chart symbols are needed. Figure 7.3 shows what such a flow chart might look like for the Order Cancellation Team, as described in Chapter Two.

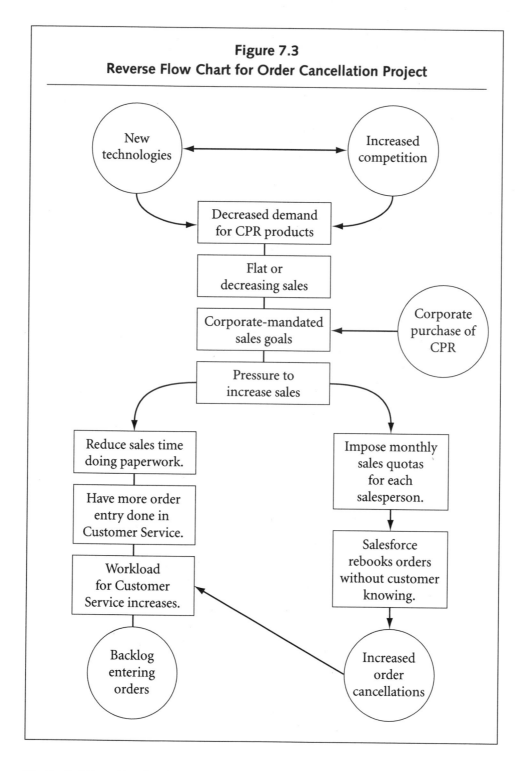

Figure 7.3
Reverse Flow Chart for Order Cancellation Project

New technologies ↔ Increased competition

Decreased demand for CPR products

Flat or decreasing sales

Corporate-mandated sales goals ← Corporate purchase of CPR

Pressure to increase sales

Reduce sales time doing paperwork.

Have more order entry done in Customer Service.

Workload for Customer Service increases.

Backlog entering orders

Impose monthly sales quotas for each salesperson.

Salesforce rebooks orders without customer knowing.

Increased order cancellations

Unlike most flow charts, this type is drawn beginning at the bottom and ending at the top.

Step 1: Draw a circle at the bottom of the chart to show the way the problem first presented itself to the team. For example, for the Order Cancellation Team there were two presenting issues: increased order cancellations and increased backlog in customer service.

Step 2: Draw a map identifying those forces or factors that influence the two presenting problems. For example, the salesperson rebooking orders without customers' knowledge is a key factor causing the increased cancellations.

Step 3: Continue drawing the map until some root cause issues are defined. These "root causes" are most often some underlying change in business realities facing the organization. For example, the Order Cancellation Team determined that there were two root causes: new technologies and increased competition.

ACTION STEP 2: REACH OUT TO INFLUENCE OTHERS

For most projects there are often many key players whose involvement in and relationships with the projects will be critical to success. They might include

- Senior executives
- Immediate managers of project team members
- Subject matter experts
- Peers of project team members
- Other project teams
- Customers
- Suppliers
- Distributors

In addition, many organizations formally designate individuals to serve as sponsors or champions for projects. Sponsors are typically managers who possess immediate and direct responsibilities for areas that are targeted by projects. Champions are usually senior managers who have proposed the projects at the executive level. The roles of sponsors and champions will be examined in more detail in Chapter Eight.

To varying degrees stakeholders can help or hinder teams. They can serve to speed up or slow down learning cycles. They can affect the depth of learning by supporting or resisting the challenging of assumptions and reframing of projects. They can influence the breadth of projects by encouraging or discouraging the widening of project scope. When it comes to their relationships with stakeholders, project teams have two basic choices. They can be reactive and passive, or they can be anticipative and proactive. From the beginning of projects, radical teams do whatever they can to manage relationships in ways that will be beneficial to their projects. They proactively seek to manage the influence of a wide range of stakeholders on their projects.

Identify the Key Players

Who are the key players? Reg Revans (1982), the founder of action learning, has suggested that three questions be asked:

- *Who knows?* (Who possesses important information?)
- *Who cares?* (Who is committed to achieving successful outcomes?)
- *Who can?* (Who has the power to take action?)

The people identified through these questions can provide potentially valuable contributions to project success. Sometimes individuals fall into all three categories. However, it is more likely that different people will be identified through each of the three questions.

APPLICATION EXERCISE 7.2: IDENTIFYING THE KEY PLAYERS

Teams can use the following exercise to identify key players and plan strategies to obtain their support for projects:

Step 1: Draw a chart like the one shown next on a flip chart or white board.

Step 2: Together, the team identifies and writes down the names of individuals who possess knowledge important to the project, placing "Xs" in the "Who Knows?" column.

Step 3: Do the same for the "Who Cares?" and "Who Can?" columns. If a name is already listed, place an "X" in the appropriate column.

Step 4: Ask the team to explore the best approach for obtaining the support of each individual on the list. Write down the actions team members will take to do so in the "Strategy to Gain Support" column.

Name	Who Knows?	Who Cares?	Who Can?	Strategy to Gain Support

Obtain Stakeholder Support

What strategies should project teams use to obtain the support of key stakeholders? It depends on the individuals in question and the reasons they might have for withholding support from a given project.

One possibility is that the project may not be a personal priority. Although it may be a priority for team members, projects are often not a priority for stakeholders. There might not be any incentive for these individuals to give time or attention to the project. In fact, there may be disincentives. For example, involvement with projects may mean more work and might take effort away from immediate job responsibilities. In such cases teams need to find ways to make support for the project a personal priority. Here are some strategies for doing that:

- *Appeal to organizational citizenship.* This approach works for many people. If they can see that they are contributing to overall organization success, they will often lend support, even if personal costs are involved.
- *Ask for signals from "on high."* Clear and unmistakable signals from top executives that projects are important can often reduce obstacles to support.
- *Rearrange personal priorities.* In organizations with tight performance goals and reward systems, the personal priorities of stakeholders may need to be formally changed by working with their managers.

- *Provide professional development.* For some individuals, obtaining new skills and knowledge is a strong incentive for offering assistance.
- *Offer visibility and recognition.* For others, obtaining increased visibility in their organizations and being recognized for their expertise will do the trick.

Another possibility is that projects are perceived as personal threats or affronts. Some stakeholders may perceive the existence of project teams as indirect or direct threats to their authority or affronts to their professional reputations. For example, they may see projects as encroaching on their areas of responsibility. They may be insulted that they were not asked to be on a team. They may have been involved in previous unsuccessful attempts to deal with the issues being addressed by the project teams. Here are some approaches that often work in such situations:

- *Be sensitive to self-esteem issues.* It is important to show genuine respect for the expertise individuals bring to projects and demonstrate honest appreciation for the contribution they make. Doing so goes a long way toward reducing the self-esteem issues that might be underlying any resistance to providing support.
- *Share the recognition.* Team members need to avoid creating any perception that they are just out for themselves. They need to make it very clear that many other individuals contributed to the projects and should share the credit for any success.
- *Establish formal roles.* Sometimes teams find it useful to establish formal roles for some stakeholders, such as subject matter experts or resource advisers.

ACTION STEP 3: LEARN FROM THE PAST

It is important that teams have access to information regarding the company's previous history that may be relevant to their projects and that teams make use of this accumulated wisdom. To make this as easy as possible, more and more companies are establishing formal systems to capture lessons learned from major projects and events and make them available to those tackling similar problems in the future. Over 50 percent of *Fortune* 500 companies now have some sort of formal "lessons learned" system (Kotnour, 1999). The next chapter describes the U.S. Army's after action review (AAR) process, which systematically captures and shares lessons learned from individual units and consolidates them for the entire army. Many leading businesses have modeled systems after the AAR process.

In most cases teams will need to do some legwork to uncover relevant historical information. Team members often possess a great deal of this information themselves, especially if teams have a diversified membership. However, members do not always share historical information, figuring it might be tangential or irrelevant to the current situations. Moreover, teams need some way to synthesize relevant historical information to make it useful to present tasks. Radical teams deliberately examine relevant historical information to enlighten their approaches to their projects.

One way to do this is to examine past projects. I cannot think of any organization that does not have a rich history of past projects. Some were successful: projects that produced better-than-expected results in less time than planned. Some were failures: computer conversions that brought the company to its knees and alienated many customers; new-product launches that were delayed to the point where marketplace advantage was lost.

What can be learned from old projects that might apply to new projects? Here are some examples:

- Common roadblocks and problems
- The best methods of communication and involvement
- How resistance will most likely be manifested
- The degree of openness to new ideas
- The ability to confront differences constructively
- The importance of realistic expectations
- That people will not support change for long if the company's reward system does not support it
- That changes are almost always more complex and take longer than imagined
- That new, unplanned events might arise that will require time and resources

Moreover, learning can be generalized from one part of the firm to another. Because organizations are complex, interrelated systems, it is likely that the new knowledge has sweeping application, even to organizational units with a remote relationship to the situation at hand.

The following exercise can be used to capture lessons from past projects and apply them in meaningful ways to current tasks.

APPLICATION EXERCISE 7.3A:
LEARNING FROM PAST PROJECTS

Think of a past project in your organization that has the most similarity to your present project. Then answer the questions that follow. There are no right or wrong answers. This activity should be completed individually by team members and then discussed afterward.

Step 1: What was the project? (Describe the purpose of the project and who was involved—job titles only.)

Step 2: How successful was the project? (Consider objective data that might point to the relative success of the project as well as your own personal perceptions.)

Step 3: What single event or incident that occurred during the project most positively affected project results?

Step 4: What key event or incident that occurred during the project most negatively affected project results?

Step 5: If the project were to be done again, what would you recommend be done to enhance the overall results?

Step 6: What are the lessons learned from this previous project that can be applied to the current project?

What should be done differently in this project from the previous project?

What should not be done at all in this project?

In addition to examining specific projects, teams often find it helpful to take a broader look at their organizations' past histories, including critical events, key people, major achievements, and significant failures, as well as external factors such as customers, competitors, marketplace changes, and economic forces. Doing so allows teams to see their projects in the context of an unfolding stream of forces and events. It enables them to perceive the pervasive and subtle strategic forces that might be influencing their projects. In some cases it increases their humility regarding what it will take to find lasting solutions.

All of these characteristics were present with the Order Cancellation Team. Over the course of the project, the team gradually recognized that the current problem was best understood in terms of an unfolding pattern of marketplace changes, with new competitors and technologies making old products obsolete. By looking at things from a historical perspective, the team could see that these changes had been gradually unfolding for well over a decade. The increase in order cancellations was merely symptomatic of the changes, complicated by what the organization did to adapt to them (such as merging with a larger, diversified publishing corporation and putting pressure on the salesforce for increased bookings).

The following exercise provides one approach for examining how historical events influence current projects.

APPLICATION EXERCISE 7.3B: CREATING A TIME LINE

Use the following steps to create a historical time line.

Step 1: Schedule a team meeting that will be devoted to developing a historical time line related to your project. In most cases participation in this meeting should not be limited to team members. Invite anybody who might possess information and perspectives regarding the past history of the company that might be relevant to the current project.

Step 2: Before the meeting, prepare a time line template that looks something like the following.

	1985	1990	1995	2000	Today
Key events (achievements, failures, and so forth)					
People					
Customers					
Competitors					
Technologies					
Industry changes					

The number of years that you list across the top of the time line can vary. Ten to twenty years is most common. The categories listed on the side can differ from those listed here. Select the categories that will elicit the most useful information.

Step 3: With everyone present at the meeting, both team members and guests, fill in the time line together, listing any items that people feel may bear direct or indirect influence on the current project.

Step 4: After the time line is completed, discuss the potential implications for the project, including the following:

- How is the current situation a manifestation of the broader forces and factors identified on the time line?

- What types of information do we need to gather that will tell us more about how these broader forces affect the project?

- Do we need to consider broadening the scope of the project? If so, how?

ACTION STEP 4: GO AGAINST THE ORGANIZATIONAL GRAIN

Paradoxically, to be of most help to their organizations project teams may need to be purposefully deviant and subversive, challenging the prevailing culture. What is culture? In simple terms, it is "the way we do things around here." At its best the culture represents the accumulated wisdom regarding what has made the firm successful over the years. However, given changing business realities, aspects of the culture may be harmful rather than helpful. Conservative, risk-aversive companies may need to become more aggressive. Internally focused companies may need to become more market-driven. Entrepreneurial companies may need to become more formal and systematic. Here is an example:

The Missed Opportunities Team

A large chemical manufacturer aggressively sought to reduce costs for over a decade. There were widespread lay-offs. The company reduced investments in market research and product development to minimum levels. Operational expenses were tightly controlled. Within this context an organizational culture developed that might be encapsulated as follows: *Always give the appearance that your primary concern is to reduce costs, even when doing so might be harmful to the company and cost more money in the long run.*

Recently the senior executive team concluded that the company was missing some major marketplace opportunities. A case in point: several direct competitors had successfully adapted their product lines for use in niche markets or applications different from their originally intended use. Several project teams were formed, each charged with investigating missed opportunities for specific products and making recommendations within six months. Team members were expected to fulfill their normal job responsibilities as usual while serving on the project teams.

A few months into the project, one of the teams came to the recognition that there was almost no market research information on which the team could base its recommendations. Whatever information the team would come up with they would have to generate through library research, Internet searches, interviews, and focus groups. Doing so would significantly increase the workload of team members. To be as efficient as possible, team members split up the tasks of gathering the needed market research information and agreed to gather at corporate headquarters for a two-day meeting to assemble and analyze the information. One of the team members, who was from a remote division, offered to bring her administrative assistant with her to corporate headquarters to help during the two-day meeting. The assistant could make the meeting more efficient and productive by keeping notes and completing whatever administrative tasks needed to be done.

To the surprise of the person making what seemed to be a logical and generous offer, several other team members immediately rejected the suggestion: "You can't do that at corporate. That's not our culture. If it got around that one of our employees was just sitting around for two days, and that we flew her in just for the meeting, it would look terrible." In response, the person who made the proposal responded: "Isn't that just the problem we are having with this project? The company is so cheap that it has invested almost no money in market research. No wonder our competitors are catching opportunities we're missing left and right. We are so afraid to look like we are spending any money that we do things that really hurt us. Let us just look at my suggestion from a pure cost-benefit perspective."

Over the next fifteen minutes the team figured out the precise costs in travel expenses and wages to bring the administrative assistant to corporate headquarters. They also estimated that the presence of the administrative assistant would conservatively allow the team to be 25 percent more productive and then translated that savings into a dollar figure by estimating each team member's "hourly rate." Bringing the assistant to the meeting would result in at least a 5:1 cost savings.

Based on the cost-benefit analysis, the project team decided to go ahead and invite the administrative assistant to come to corporate headquarters for the two-day meeting. Moreover, the team referred to this episode several times later in the project as it developed its recommendations, which included the proposal that the company make an ongoing investment in market research. The team supported this proposal with a cost-benefit analysis that detailed the estimated financial returns that should be derived from expanded market research.

One way to think of culture is as a set of organizational habits that may need to be broken. As seen in the Missed Opportunities Team, the company had fallen into a bad habit: discouraging people from spending money, even when the expenditure would produce tangible benefits to the company. In the larger scheme of things, bringing the administrative assistant to corporate was not a big issue. However, this issue was symbolic of the company culture. In this case the project team intentionally violated the company culture and in doing so helped lay the foundation for making final recommendations that would more significantly challenge the culture. Through this episode the team created a shared understanding of how aspects of the culture could be dysfunctional to the project. The team also strengthened its confidence that it was possible to question the prevailing culture without dire consequences.

Following are some guidelines designed to help teams challenge the prevailing cultures of their organizations and go against the grain to achieve desired project outcomes:

Limit Unnecessary Outside Influences

As stated earlier it is important that teams reach out and influence individuals who are critical to project success. At the same time they need to limit the degree to which they are influenced by any outside forces that will limit their ability to challenge assumptions and reframe projects. Teams need to cultivate their own minicultures that are, to some degree, countercultural. This means limiting routine, nonessential communications with others about their projects. In the early days of the reengineering movement, it was common for project teams to hole them-selves up in conference rooms for more than eight hours a day for months and months on end. They would tape newspaper on all the windows so no one could see in and, even more important, no one could see out. It is not necessary to go that far. However, it is important that teams intentionally distance themselves from influences that might inhibit the development of radical project solutions.

Carefully Control the Dissemination of Project Information

Similarly, teams need to release information regarding their projects when they are ready to and on their terms. The early communication of project information could bring organization-level resistance before a team is ready to deal with it. In the words of one team member, "We don't want to activate the company's immune system." Teams need to avoid having word spread throughout their organizations regarding what they are up to until they are ready to manage the consequences. In some cases teams might even need to reject requests for project updates at early stages in their projects.

Fly Under the Radar

Teams need to avoid actions early in their projects that will elicit organizational resistance. Often it is merely a matter of nuance and subtlety in how things are handled. For example, the Missed Opportunities Team originally discussed the need to develop a proposal and budget for conducting customer focus groups and then obtain advance approval before going out and gathering information. It was anticipated that some people might object to doing the focus groups, both on the basis of cost and necessity. After some discussion the team decided to go ahead and conduct the focus groups without seeking permission. Working with the salesforce, the team arranged for focus groups to be held at several upcoming trade shows. Team members absorbed the minimal costs associated with the focus groups into their own budgets. Before anybody who might object knew about them, the focus groups had been completed.

Establish Countercultural Team Norms

As illustrated by the Missed Opportunities Team, it is important that teams un-derstand the potential influences of organizational cultures on their projects. The most powerful antidotes to unhealthy cultural influences are concrete and specific actions. To be countercultural, these actions need to be different from the way people typically act in organizations. The best actions also tend to have symbolic importance, representing the teams' willingness to depart from the status quo.

APPLICATION EXERCISE 7.4: CHALLENGING THE CULTURE

The following exercise is designed to help teams establish norms that go against the organizational grain.

Step 1: Ask team members to imagine that they are describing what their organization is like to people who are not familiar with the company. Each person comes up with several adjectives that best describe "the way we do things around here." Examples: Conservative, ruthless, aggressive, slow to act, bureaucratic, top-down, competitive, innovative, caring.

Step 2: Team members then combine their lists, grouping together those descriptors that are similar.

Step 3: The team then goes back and discusses each characteristic and how it might have an effect—either positive or negative—on the project. For example, if the company is seen as very conservative, the team might have the tendency to reject novel ideas or suggestions in knee-jerk fashion, without giving them a fair hearing.

Step 4: For aspects of the culture that are seen as having a detrimental effect on the project, the team identifies the specific actions it will take over the course of the project to challenge the prevailing company culture as needed to achieve desired results. The team should identify concrete behaviors ("Fully explore new ideas even when there are risks involved") and not just general concepts (such as "Take risks").

Step 5: The team then develops a strategy for handling the downsides of challenging the corporate culture. In some cases it may be important that the teams be openly confrontational regarding the dysfunctional nature of the culture. In others it may be both unnecessary and dangerous to challenge the culture in any direct and obvious manner. In such cases the teams will need to determine how it will achieve desired project results without necessarily making everything it does obvious to the organization.

ACTION STEP 5: MAKE THINGS HAPPEN ELSEWHERE

As teams wrap up their projects, or even the major phases of their projects, they need to take concrete actions to ensure that their work has the broadest possible impact on their organizations. Teams need to be aggressive and entrepreneurial in making things happen elsewhere in the organization, avoiding limitations imposed by functional, divisional, or geographical boundaries. Yet teams also need to be smart and savvy. They must recognize that they might step on the toes of others who wonder why they are venturing into areas beyond the original scope of their projects. They need to be sensitive to the fact that they might be accused of self-promotion or of seeking personal visibility and recognition.

The following are some guidelines that project teams can use to broaden their impact on their organizations:

Share What Has Been Produced

Teams need to first identify the tangible products they have created. These often go beyond the final project deliverables. They might include financial analyses, market data, new procedures, new production methods, new forms, new vendors, and cost reduction ideas, among others. Then teams need to identify who in the organization might use these products. They might be other managers in their business unit, other business units, and other project teams.

It is important to go beyond the traditional dog-and-pony presentations that project teams often make, or are asked to make, at the end of projects. Like showing pictures from a vacation, such presentations are not very meaningful to those who were not on the trip. Here are some suggestions for sharing your work with others:

- *Make the process a two-way exchange.* Acknowledge that there might be valuable information to be passed in both directions. Besides being true, doing so will help others be open to considering how your work might be applied.

- *Focus your exchange on what will be useful and highlight the benefits.* Do more than just provide a general description of the work completed by the team. Target specific actions others can take and the positive results of doing so.

- *Recognize that others will need to make your work their own.* Encourage others to adapt and customize what you have done to fit their own situations.

- *Do not worry that others will steal your credit.* It is likely that, in the long term, those who unselfishly work to improve the organization will eventually receive the visibility and recognition they deserve.

Share What Has Been Learned

Probably the most important products that teams create are the new understandings that are generated over the course of projects. These are much harder to share than the tangible products are. To do so, teams need to openly describe to others the learning process they went through: identifying assumptions, gathering objective data and information to confirm or disconfirm the assumptions, and modifying their understandings as a result. Teams can then guide others in exploring the potential implications of what has been learned to benefit the broader organization.

As described in more detail in the next chapter, the U.S. Army's after action review (AAR) process uses the following six-step process for identifying lessons learned (Baird, Holland, and Deacon, 1999):

- *Step 1:* What was the intent? Begin by going back and defining the original purpose and goal of the action.
- *Step 2:* What happened? Describe as specifically and objectively as possible what actually occurred.
- *Step 3:* What have we learned? Identify the key information, knowledge, and insights that were gained as a result.
- *Step 4:* What do we do now? Determine what will be done as a result of what has been learned, dividing the actions into three categories: short-term, mid-term, and long-term.
- *Step 5:* Take action.
- *Step 6:* Tell someone else. Share what's been learned with anybody in the organization who might benefit.

Even if your company does not require that you complete a project postmortem, it is important that your team take the initiative to do so on its own. The team should

- Meet as soon as possible after the project is completed, while the details are still fresh.

- Involve as many people as possible who might have relevant perspectives regarding your project, including sponsors, champions, and other stakeholders.

- Conduct the lessons-learned debriefing in a climate of openness, trust, and respect. Clearly state at the outset that the purpose is not to place blame but to identify what has been learned and to make this knowledge and insight available to others in the organization.

Take the Initiative to Make Things Happen

It is important that project teams do more than merely share what has been produced and learned over the course of their projects. They need to take the initiative to make things happen in areas beyond the original scope of the projects. Here are some suggestions:

- *Always do what is best for the organization.* If your motives are always to produce the most good for the organization, your team should not have any major problems when it seeks to broaden your impact on the organization.

- *Solicit help from others.* Champions, sponsors, and others who possess a great deal of organizational experience and knowledge can steer you around political minefields that you cannot see. In many cases, they can make major hurdles look small. On the other hand, when there are major impediments, they can help you work through those as well.

- *Work with people, not around them.* Teams can quickly get into trouble if they do not inform and involve others who have legitimate roles and responsibilities.

- *Be willing to pass things off.* In some cases other groups or individuals might be more appropriate to continue the work. It does not matter who does the work or gets the credit. What is important is that the work of your project teams has the broadest possible impact on your organization.

APPLICATION EXERCISE 7.5: CREATING AN IMPACT PLAN

The following is an exercise that teams can use at the end of projects to develop a plan to maximize their impact on the whole organization:

Step 1: Draw or ask someone to draw a simple grid on a flip chart with three columns: What? Who? How?

Step 2: As a whole team, fill in the grid, working horizontally from left to right as follows:

- In Column 1, identify key products and learnings produced by the team.
- In Column 2, list various individuals, teams, or business units that might be able to benefit from the products and learnings.
- In Column 3, identify specific actions the team can take that will best ensure that each product and learning has impact on the individuals, groups, and business units listed.

What?	Who?	How?
What have we produced or learned as a team?	Who might benefit?	How can we have the most impact?

This chapter presented five action steps for increasing the speed of learning of project teams:

Action Step 1: Uncover connections.

Action Step 2: Reach out to influence others.

Action Step 3: Learn from past projects.

Action Step 4: Go against the organizational grain.

Action Step 5: Make things happen elsewhere.

The next chapter describes various types of support that organizations need to provide to help project teams be successful.

Support for Radical Project Teams

*One cannot ask others to learn something new
if one has not learned something new oneself.*

Edgar Schein[1]

*Help was there when we needed it. If we didn't need any help,
fine. It was up to us. We knew the wind was at our backs
throughout the project. The organization was behind us.
All the support we wanted was there. All we had to do was ask.*

From a team member's log

This chapter describes the support needed to successfully implement the radical project team approach in organizations. This support can be divided into two categories: soft support and hard support. Soft support deals with the intangible but very important support provided by those in leadership positions, including creating a sense of urgency, serving as role models, and helping teams overcome obstacles. Hard support refers to the formal structures and systems that organizations use to deploy the radical team approach, including methods for identifying projects, selecting members, and training teams. Individual teams can adopt the radical team approach without necessarily requiring formal structures and systems to support them. However, hard support is needed if organizations wish to scale-up their use of the radical team approach to the extent that a critical mass of teams are using the approach in a consistent and effective manner.

Most of the topics discussed in this chapter—leadership support, team training, and team member selection—apply to all teams, not just radical teams. Many books, articles, and seminars cover these topics in detail. But this chapter focuses on the key ways in which radical teams require different types of support than other teams do. As might be expected, support issues are even more critical for radical teams than with other, more traditional, types.

SOFT SUPPORT: LEADERSHIP SUPPORT FOR RADICAL TEAMS

I am using the term *leaders* to refer to people in any one of the following roles, whether they are formally designated as serving in these roles or assume them informally: *champions, sponsors, team leaders,* or *subject matter experts.*

Champions are usually senior-level managers within the business units or divisions in which project teams operate. Champions are often the ones who first propose projects and usually serve as the primary advocates for projects from the beginning to the end. In some cases groups collectively serve as champions (such as senior management teams and other committees). Champions are often the ones who are best able to articulate the long-term importance of projects to businesses, seeing a direct connection between projects and strategic business plans and objectives. At the beginning of projects, champions generally seek to communicate to project teams the end results that are to be achieved. They then empower teams to carry out the projects. Champions typically have limited involvement in projects as they are under way, except for obtaining periodic updates at key points or helping resolve problems that might threaten project success. Champions are also involved with prioritizing projects within organizations and allocating resources (financial, people, and other resources) to the most critical projects.

Sponsors are generally mid-level or senior managers who possess management responsibilities for areas most directly related to specific projects. It is their job to work directly with project teams, providing whatever support is needed during projects. They are the first persons teams turn to when impediments arise.

Team leaders are members of teams who are designated to serve in leadership capacities. Not all projects have team leaders. This role is often shared collectively by teams and rotated among members. Project team leaders usually operate as facilitative leaders, with responsibilities for key decisions made by the whole team. They schedule and plan meetings, keep records, and otherwise provide support for their project teams.

Subject matter experts are individuals who have the content expertise that project teams need. They are not team members and do not participate in team decisions.

The way these leadership roles are handled varies greatly from organization to organization. Some firms formally designate people to fulfill each of the roles listed; others might identify only a few; still others might not formally establish any of the roles. There is no one best way. Each organization needs to develop a system that works for it. What is important is that the roles are understood and fulfilled effectively.

At the heart of this book are the stories of five radical teams, identified through a comparative analysis of the speed, depth, and breadth of learning of twenty teams. Each team was selected as "best in class" when compared to other teams that were started at the same time and received the same instructions and guidance. In every one of these cases key contributions were made by those in leadership capacities that helped make the projects successful. Here are brief illustrations from each of the five teams.

The Order Cancellation Team (Chapter Two)

At the beginning of the project the vice president of operations—the team's informally designated sponsor—made it clear that he expected the team to come up with a fundamentally different way to look at the problem, given the fact that several other teams had tackled it and failed. At the first meeting he reinforced the critical importance of the project to the success of the company, pointing to direct financial losses and unfavorably comparing the company's performance to other corporate business units. When the team began uncovering some potentially embarrassing facts, he worked quietly behind the scenes with the senior management team, ensuring that no one would be surprised or blindsided by the team's recommendations.

The North American Consolidation Team (Chapter Three)

Although he did not show it at the time, the general manager, serving as the overall project champion, later confessed that he was taken aback when the Marketing Team presented an update that suggested that the overall consolidation did not make sense. Despite the fact that the other teams all supported the direction, he listened carefully and encouraged everyone to reserve judgment and hear what the team had to say. In front of the whole group he admitted that the overall direction he had provided the group was wrong. In the middle of the project he announced that there would be a fundamental change of course; they would adopt the recommendations of the Marketing Team and abandon his own plan.

The Cost Reduction Team (Chapter Five)

A key incident occurred about halfway through the project when team members held a meeting with their designated sponsor, the division manager. The team was fully convinced that it had gone as far as it could go. It was prepared to call the project complete, thinking it had found every possible way to reduce costs. The team's sponsor sent the team back to the drawing board with the call to find "a different way of thinking and working" and not to worry about being embarrassed about admitting the need to change. Before doing so, he told a brief personal anecdote, giving an example of a practice he had endorsed for years that now, in retrospect, was clearly an unnecessary and costly expense to the company. When introducing the team before it presented its recommendations to a room of about a hundred people, including the executive vice president of the corporation (the project champion), the division manager got up and told the same anecdote.

The Mathematics Improvement Team (Chapter Six)

Throughout the project, the school's principal served as both champion and sponsor, meeting with the Mathematics Improvement Team to receive updates on the project and to see how she could help. In each meeting she reinforced the need for the school as a whole—every teacher, every administrator, and every parent—to critically examine the process of teaching and learning in the school and what each person could do to improve things. She said that she had no preconceived answers and was looking for only one result: dramatic and immediate improvement in how well students were learning mathematics. She reinforced that no individual was at fault but that somehow the school as a whole was not meeting the needs of its children. She quietly secured the funds needed by the team to purchase materials and hire an external person to do staff development. She never asked for or received any specific information about the teaching performance of individual teachers from the professor who observed each teacher in the classroom, making it safe for teachers to examine and change their practices without fear of judgment.

The Production Scheduling Team (Chapter Seven)

During this project there were two key times when the team requested a meeting with the executive committee. Before the first meeting the members of the executive committee agreed among themselves to limit themselves to asking questions while the team was still in the room, not giving any opinions or rendering any decisions. This allowed the executive committee to freely hash out the issues behind closed doors and then speak with a single, unified voice to the team. This process also enabled executive committee members to undergo a learning process themselves, just as the team was going through its own learning process. Several executive committee members changed their opinions as a result. When the team received word from the executive committee that they were to expand the scope of the project, members were happily surprised, having suspected that one or more executive committee members wanted to keep the project contained. The second time the team met with the executive committee, the committee found it harder to stick to the same disciplined approach, likely because the team was now making concrete recommendations that would significantly alter how the company did business. However, after the team left, the committee regrouped itself and held several meetings over the course of the next week before approving the team's recommendations.

GUIDELINES FOR EFFECTIVE LEADERSHIP

In looking at these illustrations, it is possible to extract several important guidelines for effective leadership support of radical teams. I describe these in the sections that follow.

Create a Sense of Urgency

Leaders supporting radical teams demonstrate a consistent and passionate commitment to fundamental change. They set a clear expectation that they will not be satisfied with anything less than dramatic improvements and new ways of doing business. They avoid using abstract conceptual arguments to support the need for change, such as describing the general forces of deregulation, competition, or globalization. Instead they make compelling business cases by marshaling concrete and objective supporting evidence that creates a sense of immediacy among team members. According to Kurt Lewin (1951), all organizations experience relatively long periods in which they are "frozen," remaining stable and secure, committed to retaining the status quo. Leaders "unfreeze" teams by establishing a strong expectation and irrefutable case for change.

For example, the division manager who served as the sponsor for the Cost Reduction Team was able to demonstrate on a spreadsheet that, as a result of deregulation, the company would soon be facing competitors who had less than half the company's direct costs per kilowatt hour. Only by slashing repair costs, among other costs, could the company begin to compete. The principal in the Mathematics Improvement Project did much the same thing. She demonstrated that similar schools with similar students were performing at least 50 percent better than were their school's students and made it clear that this situation had to change.

Create Safe Environments

At the same time, these leaders recognized that team learning requires that teams operate in a climate that encourages members to admit that they do not have the answers; to let go of long-held beliefs; to experiment, make errors, and learn from the errors; and to openly question the status quo. A major factor determining the degree to which safety exists, or is perceived to exist, is the support provided by leaders.

Telling teams that it is safe to engage in these behaviors is not enough, although several of the leaders we observed could not resist giving a "think out of the box" speech at the beginning of projects. What leaders do as projects progress is more important. Teams watch carefully for signs that indicate how secure it is to take risks. They look at what leaders actually do, not what they say. They watch who gets rewarded and who gets punished and for what reasons. They test the water by taking low-level, calculated risks. They gauge whether they are being set up by being put in no-win situations in which needed resources, coaching, and help will not be provided. In these cases, it is how the leaders act, often on the spur of the moment, that serves as the key indicator to team members whether it is truly safe or not. The most effective leaders carefully watch the subtle signals they are sending to their teams. The executive committee in the case of the Production Scheduling Team did just that when it carefully controlled its responses the two times the team tested the water by confronting the executive committee regarding the purpose and scope of the project.

Serve as a Learning Role Model

The best way to create a safe environment is for leaders to be role models for the types of learning behaviors they expect their teams to exhibit. Some specific things they can do to create a safe environment are to

- Acknowledge their own ignorance.
- Present any perspectives that they have as assumptions to be looked into rather than facts to be treated as givens.
- Demonstrate their own abilities to change their thinking and reframe their understandings of projects.

This was shown in the case of the Cost Reduction Team, when the division manager was willing to risk embarrassing himself before putting his team members in a situation where they might be embarrassed. It was also exhibited by the North American Consolidation Team, when the general manager admitted in front of a room full of people that he had been wrong.

Ask Lots of Good Questions

A key way to be a role model for learning is to demonstrate strong inquiry skills. As described earlier in the book, inquiry is more than just asking questions. It is being genuinely open to the influence of others and to discovering new knowledge and insights. Here is how one sponsor described her recognition of the importance of inquiry to being a leader of radical teams:

> The questioning process is something I had forgotten. Years ago, I was a leader in a Great Books Discussion Group. There the role of the leader is to question—not to make any judgment of what is being said. Instead, I tried to bring about discussion and discovery by posing questions to get people to think critically. I realized that that's what I needed to be doing with my teams.

Coach Teams Through the Rough Spots

During the course of most projects, there are a few critical points at which everything seems to explode. Teams lose sight of what they are trying to accomplish. They make things more complex than they need to be. At these points, those in leadership roles can serve a useful function by helping to simplify the situation, focusing the teams on the most critical issues, and guiding them in taking some constructive next steps that will begin moving them ahead again. The examples provided earlier show how the most successful teams were blessed with the wise and judicious counsel of leaders who knew just when to step in, knew exactly what help was needed, and then stepped out, making sure that the teams still retained ownership and accountability for their projects.

Help Manage the Politics

By their very nature, radical project teams are going to ruffle some feathers before projects are complete. If not, they are likely not doing their jobs. Those in leadership roles, especially champions and sponsors, often possess a wealth of knowledge about organizational politics that team members do not. They understand how far the limits can be pushed. They know when windows of opportunity are open and when they are closed. During projects, leaders need to help teams navigate through the sometimes-treacherous waters of organizational politics. Much of what leaders do is not visible to their teams. It is done quietly behind the scenes. Their aim is to give the teams the space needed to be successful. Yet they do not cushion their teams from understanding the complex realities that exist in organizations. Over the course of projects the most effective leaders also seek to develop the capabilities of teams to manage these realities on their own, without the intervention of others. With the Order Cancellation Project, the vice president of operations worked carefully behind the scenes to make sure that the team's recommendations would not come as a total surprise to other senior managers.

HARD SUPPORT: SYSTEMS AND STRUCTURES
TO SUPPORT RADICAL TEAMS

Let us now turn to the type of structures and systems organizations frequently develop to support radical teams in their organizations. The organization of these structures and systems may be highly formal and rigid or fairly informal and flexible. Much depends on organizational context, including the size of the firm, the nature of the business, and the types of projects that are involved. Here are two very different contexts in which radical teamwork approaches have been successfully implemented.

A Large Financial Services Institution

This firm is struggling to keep up with the quickening pace of change in the financial services industry. Over the past year, radical project teams have become the primary vehicles for doing so.

The organization is divided into six divisions. Once each month, the division leaders (called the leadership team) meet to determine the need for project teams, to obtain updates from in-progress teams, to review and approve project team recommendations, and to oversee the implementation of recommendations from past project teams. The projects run the gamut. Some deal with marketing issues, others with product and service issues, and still others with internal operations. At any given time, six to twelve project teams may be active.

As a first step for each project the leadership team creates a first draft of a project team charter. The charter is a one-page document that describes the project's purpose, goals, deliverables, time line, available resources, and other relevant issues. The leadership team also designates a project sponsor (usually a senior manager or middle manager), a project team leader (someone who has successfully served on project teams in the past and who has received some training in leading project teams), and, when needed, subject matter experts (people who have knowledge relevant to the project but are not members of the project team).

The sponsor and the team leader then recruit project team members. In doing so they try to achieve a balance between the number of people who have expertise or a vested interest in the project and the number who are more removed from the project and can bring a fresh eye to it. (As a rule of thumb, half of the team members should be relatively uninformed about the project area.) In selecting team members, the sponsor and team leader also seek representatives from various functional areas such as operations, marketing, and information systems. When making their selections they consider the personal development goals of team members. Ideally, working on the project should help team members achieve these personal development goals, such as gaining experience in areas of the business in which they have no background.

The project begins with a one-day kick-off training session facilitated by the firm's project coordinator and attended by the whole team and its sponsor. More than one team can attend the training session at the same time; however, individual teams sit together because much of the training session consists of hands-on working sessions in which each team does some initial work on its project.

At the beginning of the training session the sponsor is asked to briefly present the team charter, as developed by the leadership team. The project team then identifies any questions it has for the leadership team regarding the charter and any changes it would recommend. The team is then asked to establish ground rules for how it wants to work together, using a process similar to the one described earlier in this book. The team generates a list of assumptions it has about the project and identifies a series of quick actions it can take over the next week or two to test the validity of these assumptions. Toward the end of the workshop, the project coordinator introduces the Project Team Tool Kit, which consists of a three-ring binder containing several exercises similar to the application exercises presented throughout this book. The project coordinator tells the team that he or she will be available if the team would like mini-training sessions during the project on how to use the exercises in the tool kit.

A Small Medical Products Manufacturer

The company has made a name for itself by coming up with revolutionary new products faster than anybody in the business. It uses radical project teams to explore new technologies, develop new products based on these technologies, and bring these products to market. Success is driven by two factors: being market-driven and getting product to market fast.

A shopping list of projects is established at an annual strategic planning retreat. Just about everybody in the company attends the retreat, as do some key customers. Market information is assembled and distributed beforehand, including focus group summaries, customer surveys, and market analyses. During the year, it is up to the new-product development committee (made up of the company president, the vice president of technology, the vice president of marketing, and three members from different functional areas who rotate on and off the committee each year) to update the project list as needed, shifting priorities and adding projects as new market information becomes available. For high-priority projects, the new-product development committee designates a person from the research and development staff to handle the start-up of the project. It is up to that person to recruit a cross-functional team, which will assume overall responsibility for the project. As a first step, the team has a kick-off meeting in which it writes its own charter, develops ground rules, and identifies original project assumptions. Over the course of the project, the team meets periodically with the new-product development committee to review project status. There are no sponsors. Each team can choose whether to designate a project team leader or not. The team can also have different people serve as a project team leader for various phases of the project.

When the radical project team concept was introduced a few years ago, several training sessions were held for everyone in the company. These sessions were structured as hands-on project simulations, in which teams were formed and guided through the various steps in completing a simulated (although very realistic) project. During this training, several exercises, similar to the application exercises described in this book, were introduced. Since then, periodic training sessions have been held for new employees. On a rotating basis members of previous project teams lead the training sessions and share what they have learned about what worked and what did not work with the process.

GUIDELINES FOR LEADERSHIP

Each of these organizations provides support for radical project teams, but they do so in very different ways. One does so in a formal and structured fashion. The other is more flexible and informal. Yet they both adhere to the guidelines I describe in the sections to follow.

Identifying and Defining Projects

Follow these guidelines when identifying and defining radical team projects.

Select Projects That Require Radical Teamwork. Organizations that anticipate the extensive use of radical teams need to establish some mechanism for determining the types of projects for which radical teamwork is needed. As noted earlier, not all projects require radical teamwork. However, given changes in business realities, more and more organizations are facing problems and tasks for which traditional forms of teamwork and project management will not be successful.

Earlier in the book several criteria were proposed for determining the need for radical teams:

- Dramatic results and extensive improvements in performance are being called for.

- These are new or unknown situations the companies have not faced before.

- One or more unsuccessful attempts have been made to solve these problems in the past.

- The problems are linked to a broad range of other organizational issues and factors.

The specific procedure for selecting projects can vary widely. Whatever method is used, it is important that those selecting projects can clearly articulate the features of a project that make it appropriate for the radical team approach. Some organizations establish a steering committee to handle project selection and also serve as overall champion for projects. This committee might then use a standard checklist such as the one presented in Chapter Five to determine the degree to which projects meet the criteria. Other organizations keep the process more informal, with projects being proposed and accepted on an as-needed basis.

Define Projects in Terms of End Results. When projects are initially defined, it is essential that they be expressed in terms of end results and not the means for achieving them. Many project teams struggle because embedded within the definition of their projects are direct or indirect indications of what the solutions should be. One technique to test whether projects are defined in terms of final outcomes is to ask the following question: *If I were to leave the organization and come back in two or three years, how would business results be different as a result of the work of this project team?*

Let us take as an example a public utility that provides both gas and electric service. Currently, when the company is required to go to a property and identify (markout) existing underground gas and electric lines, two different crews need to be sent to the site. Recently, the company established a project team to do the following:

Purpose: To recommend a method by which mark-outs for gas and electric can be completed at the same time.

Using the question just posed, it becomes clear that the purpose statement does not reflect business results but the means to achieve business results. A more useful purpose statement would read as follows:

Purpose: To recommend a method of reducing the costs of doing mark-outs.

By stating the purposes of teams in terms of business outcomes, teams will be more likely to explore a broader variety of potential solutions and also avoid rushing to single, predetermined answers.

Set High Expectations. In most organizations today, people are expected to do what it takes to get things done. Therefore, team members are often expected to complete project responsibilities while fulfilling all or a significant part of their current job responsibilities. If you are a champion, a sponsor, or the immediate manager of a project team member, there is nothing wrong with having high expectations regarding the ability of project team members to balance regular work responsibilities with project responsibilities. Setting ambitious time lines and targets for project completion is also important to propel teams forward as quickly as possible.

Yet there is a limit to how high expectations should go. Let us say that a team member's next-level manager has little interest in the project and fully expects the team member to "do his job" exactly as he would have if the project did not exist. Moreover, this next-level manager is the person conducting the team member's annual performance review and is the key person in determining raises and bonuses. As a result, this team member might be put in a no win situation. It is important that individuals not be provided with two conflicting sets of expectations (one from the "job" and one from the "project") that are beyond their capabilities to deal with. Moreover, completion of project responsibilities should be integrated into any existing performance and reward system.

Selecting Team Members

Having the right make-up of teams is critical to project success. In most cases team members should have the choice as to whether they are on teams or not. However, this cannot always be the case. For projects that are truly mission-critical, there is a good chance that at least a few team members will be indispensable. Persons who recruit members for radical teams need to be very deliberate in choosing team members to ensure that the right mix of skills, perspectives, and personalities is achieved. Here are some factors that should be considered when recruiting and selecting team members:

Seek Diversity in All Its Forms. Even more than with traditional project teams, diversity among team members is important, including cultural diversity, gender diversity, functional diversity (team members possessing differing backgrounds and skill sets), seniority diversity (some old-time employees mixed with some newer employees), business unit diversity (members representing the various divisions of the organization), and learning style diversity (mixing planning-oriented people with action-oriented people, and so on). Diversity is essential because it reduces the likelihood that team members will share the same assumptions and preconceptions about projects. Diversity is important because it increases the degree to which teams will be reflective of their larger organizational systems. Diversity may also provide a broad set of skills and perspectives that teams can draw on when investigating. For these reasons, diverse teams are more likely to challenge assumptions, reframe projects, and broaden their impact on their organizations.

Avoid Selecting Members with Strong Personal Stakes or Rigid Preconceptions. Sometimes people are too close to projects to be able to engage in the learning process that is the core of the radical project team approach. They may be unwilling to consider possibilities and options other than those they bring to the project. They may have too much personal interest in ensuring that projects turn out one way or another. If that is the case (and it is always a judgment call), these individuals should not be selected as team members. If they possess knowledge or expertise that is critical to projects, they could be designated to serve as subject matter experts.

Select a Few Naive (But Very Smart) People. The term *naive* in this case refers to people who possess limited experience or background directly related to the projects at hand. They might be from other business units, represent other functional areas, or be relatively new to their companies. As a result they should be able to approach projects with limited biases and preconceptions. Although naive when it comes to the projects, they should also be logical, quick thinkers—people who pick up on things fast and, maybe most important, ask the "dumb" questions that might not be asked otherwise.

Make Sure Members Possess Basic Team and Project Skills. This is not the time to develop fundamental skills in working in teams and managing projects. Although team members do not have to be experts, they should be able to be productive team members from the beginning of projects. They should have sound communication skills, understand what makes team meetings effective, and be able to handle conflict without becoming personal and disruptive. They should also know something about how to manage projects, including how to set goals, develop project plans, obtain the help and support of other people, and meet deadlines and commitments.

Use Projects as Opportunities for Professional Development. The sorts of projects talked about in this book provide ideal opportunities to foster the development of team members. In many cases they will be able to acquire a broader, more encompassing understanding of their organizations, develop expertise in functional areas in which they have little previous background, and obtain experience tackling strategic business problems often reserved for senior managers. Ideally, when setting up project teams, leaders should discuss with individual team members how attainment of their personal development goals could be advanced through work on the projects. In actuality, participation in a team often acts as a form of assessment center for high-potential individuals, providing them with the chance to demonstrate skills and capabilities that they might have no other opportunity to showcase.

Training Radical Teams

Earlier I described how two companies implemented the radical project team approach in different ways. The two firms were similar in that both provided training to project teams.

Train Teams, Not Individuals. In most organizations, project management training is provided to individuals rather than teams. Typically the company has a standard course in project management, and people are expected to take this course sometime during their careers. It is assumed that, because individual team members have participated in the training at some point in time, the teams will be more effective when the time comes to work on projects.

Think about a different approach. Rather than training individuals, train teams as collective units. Team members attend the training together and at key points during the workshop actually apply what they have learned directly to their projects. In most cases this is a much more powerful approach. The training is immediately applied and is therefore perceived as relevant and important. The training is specifically focused on what project teams need. It represents an efficient use of time because teams complete important project work during the training workshop. Maybe most important, it also ensures that team members receive a consistent and uniform message regarding how the process should work.

There are a few potential roadblocks with this approach. For example, only one project team might need training at a particular time. I have not found holding sessions for individual teams to be a problem. It is often possible to recruit some members of previous teams to serve as trainers for new teams, and with a little coaching they generally do a great job. Soon it is possible to have a small cadre of trainers on tap to provide training as needed. Another potential roadblock occurs when those who have been trained previously are asked to come to training again in relationship to a new project. Again, in practice this is less of a problem than it might first appear. Because the training sessions consist of teams doing real work on their real projects, people have generally not objected to attending multiple kick-off workshops. In addition, when individuals are encouraged to share their past experiences working on projects, it serves the dual purpose of enriching the training for the new trainees and recognizing the expertise of the experienced team members.

Provide Standard Start-Up Training. It is often very useful for organizations to establish a standard kick-off training process for project teams. This training is focused on key start-up tasks such as clarifying the purposes, goals, and deliverables of the projects; establishing team ground rules; and developing initial project plans. Figure 8.1 provides a typical outline for such a kick-off workshop.

A basic kick-off workshop can usually be completed in a day and a half to two days. Sometimes sessions extend longer if additional training content needs to be covered. For example, in some organizations additional training is provided that covers the company's specific project management system, including any relevant procedures and forms. In other organizations training in project management software or groupware might be included.

Figure 8.1
Sample Agenda of Kick-Off Workshop

I. Radical Teams: An Introduction

   A. The changing nature of business projects

   B. Traditional project teams versus radical project teams

   C. Case examples of radical project teams

II. Project Team Ground Rules

   A. Definition and examples of team ground rules

   B. Team breakout sessions (Each team establishes a set of ground rules regarding how it wants to operate as a team.)

III. Project Team Charter

   A. Purpose of a project team charter and an example

   B. Team breakout session

      1. The project team sponsor presents a draft of the project team charter.

      2. Each team develops questions and suggested changes to the charter.

IV. Approaching Projects as a Learning Process

   A. The team learning cycle

   B. Three ways to accelerate learning: speed, depth, breadth

   C. Project team case study example

V. Surfacing Assumptions

   A. Definition of assumptions and some examples

   B. Team breakout session

      1. Each team identifies assumptions about the project.

      2. Each team brainstorms specific actions that can be taken to test the validity of assumptions.

      3. Each team develops an initial project plan, defining the specific action steps that will be taken to begin the project.

Provide Additional Training on a Just-In-Time Basis. Many organizations tend to provide training that tries to cover all aspects of teamwork or project management in a single dose. From my experience the best approach to training teams in the radical project team approach is the just-in-time training method. Just-in-time training involves giving teams just enough initial training during the kick-off workshop to start their projects. Then at key points during projects, additional training is made available on a just-in-time basis. This approach can be used to provide training in many of the methods associated with traditional project management, such as techniques for gathering information (structured interviewing, conducting focus groups, and developing and implementing written survey questionnaires), analyzing risks, and developing presentations. Training is usually much more powerful if it is provided immediately before the time the teams will use the skills.

The just-in-time approach can also be used effectively with the tools and techniques presented in this book. For example, at the end of kick-off workshops, trainers might provide teams with a listing of available tools and exercises presented in this book, describing their purpose, how they are used, and when they are used. The Quick Guide to Application Exercises at the end of the book provides more detailed information regarding when teams might use each of these techniques. After being introduced to a series of tools and exercises at the beginning of their projects, teams are able to select which techniques and exercises might be helpful at various points in their project. In many cases teams can use these tools without additional help, especially if members of the team have been members of radical project teams in the past. However, help from outside trainers or coaches may sometimes be useful. Many organizations tell their project teams that trainers are available to assist them in the use of any of the tools if they would like additional help.

Integrate Training and Project Work. Whenever training is provided and whatever that training is, the training will be most effective if it is integrated with teams doing real work on their real projects. Training sessions, therefore, consist of providing brief "bites" of instruction, immediately followed by direct application to projects. After each bite, teams stop for a working session in which they complete key project tasks, applying what they have just learned. This approach is reflected in the outline of the kick-off training session presented in Figure 8.1. For example, after learning about the purpose and elements of a team charter, teams immediately go into breakout sessions in which they critique their own team's charter and suggest possible changes.

Establish a Lessons-Learned System. One of the best ways to help teams acquire the knowledge they need to successfully complete their projects is through a lessons-learned system. Such a system provides a standardized and structured method by which future teams can learn from teams that have gone before them. It also provides a mechanism for organizations to draw some overall conclusions about what works and what does not work across a range of different teams and projects over a period of time. More and more organizations are establishing lessons-learned systems, which include

- A standardized protocol for conducting project team debriefings (postmortems)
- A means of storing lessons learned for future recall
- A means for retrieving lessons learned by teams either at the start of or during their projects

In many cases lessons-learned systems also require that teams submit copies of key project documents, including final reports.

As mentioned in the last chapter, many lessons-learned systems have been patterned after the U.S. Army's after action review (AAR) process. Here is a more complete description of the process.

After Action Reviews

Probably the most sophisticated approach to capturing and sharing lessons learned between groups and across an entire organization is the U.S. Army's AAR.[2] This process has been adapted for use by many leading organizations, including Chrysler, British Petroleum, and Analog Devices. The AAR occurs by bringing together as many people as possible who have perspectives on an event immediately after any key actions have been completed to review what happened, identify lessons learned, and most important, take action as a result.

The foundation of the AAR is the establishment of a standardized, simple series of steps that is used anytime an AAR is conducted, no matter at what level of the army.

Step 1: What was the intent?

Step 2: What happened?

Step 3: What have we learned?

Step 4: What do we do now?

Step 5: Take action.

Step 6: Tell someone else.

Most AARs are relatively brief, often no more than fifteen to thirty minutes in length and rarely more than an hour.

The power of the AAR process is that it provides for an integrated structure by which lessons learned at individual units of the army are gradually "rolled up" to produce broader and broader insights for the whole army. For example, when troops were sent to Haiti several years ago, the first units used the AAR process to identify several key lessons learned: that the eighty-pound backpacks carried by troops were too heavy, that troops needed more water, and that more intravenous tubes were needed to deal with dehydration and illnesses. These lessons learned were quickly disseminated to the units that were coming in the next wave. The isolated lessons learned by separate units were consolidated at command levels, which were able to determine that problems were all caused by an underlying issue—if troops carried lighter backpacks, they would not need as much water or dehydrate as quickly.

Various business organizations have built their own systems loosely based on the army's AAR. For example, Analog Devices has created a four-level AAR process that is used by all new-product development teams:

Level 1: Within Teams. Weekly meetings are held to track progress on various product development projects. Each team completes a one-page form answering the six AAR questions.

Level 2: Across Teams. Once every six weeks, team leaders of the various teams meet together and share lessons learned that might be helpful to other teams, as well as to the organization as a whole.

Level 3: With Customers. Periodically, the same process is used with key customers as a means of strengthening customer relationships.

Level 4: Across Divisions. An AAR is completed on each new product one year after the product has gone into production. The lessons learned are then used to improve the new-product development process.

There are many different types of lessons-learned systems. Some are high-tech, relying on Internet, intranet, or groupware for storage and retrieval. Some are high-touch, providing face-to-face means for teams to get together and share what they have learned. Most are a combination of the two. Ernst & Young recently conducted a study of a range of different lessons-learned systems, including those of

Ford Motor Company, Chevron, and British Petroleum.[3] The study concluded that the best systems are kept simple, with the minimal structure needed to keep them going. They usually start with a few small pilot programs and evolve over time.

What lessons are shared through a lessons-learned system? They vary greatly. Some can be quantitative data (such as financial information, technical data, research results, market statistics, and benchmarking data). Some can be knowledge obtained as a result of projects (such as supplier and source information, competitor information, and project management tools and techniques). And some can be subjective insights (roadblocks and problems and how to overcome them, what makes teams successful, perceptions of the organizational culture). Although teams could possibly obtain this information on their own, a lessons-learned system reduces the need for teams to engage in the time-consuming task of reconstructing what has been done in the past.

One of the most exciting uses of a lessons-learned system is to track teams from a team learning perspective. Several leading organizations are including an analysis of the speed, depth, and breadth of team learning as part of the postmortems completed and submitted by teams. In much the way we did with the twenty teams described in this book, each organization can then establish its own database of radical teams, identifying teams with the greatest speed, depth, and breadth of learning and teams that have produced the most significant breakthrough results. The stories of these teams can be chronicled and shared with future teams. I cannot think of a better and more powerful way of spreading the radical team approach through an organization.

This chapter completes Part Two of the book, which has focused on putting the radical project team approach into action. The next and final chapter offers a conclusion designed to help you make the most use of what has been presented throughout the book.

Conclusion
The Personal Side of Radical Teams

As this book ends, I hope you feel you are taking away a solid grasp of the radical team framework. In other words I hope you see the importance of reframing projects, have the ability to view the work of project teams as a learning process, and know how to assess the learning of project teams on three dimensions: speed, depth, and breadth. I also hope you have acquired the ability to begin putting the radical project team approach into action, applying the specific action steps described in the second half of the book. This last chapter will guide you in exploring what it means to be a member of a radical team.

It is not uncommon that people look back after five or ten years and remember in vivid detail what it was like to be a member of a radical team. They tell war stories. They point to their experiences on such teams as defining moments in their careers, providing skills and knowledge that have led to bigger and better things. They also describe how they grew as individuals, becoming less sure that they have all of the answers and becoming more sensitive and open to others with different perspectives. In fact, the relationships developed among radical team members often endure well after projects end and often last for entire careers.

However, radical teams are not for everyone. Whereas some people find their experiences enriching and motivating, others find them confusing and frustrating. This chapter will help you determine whether the radical team concept fits your own personal characteristics. It will also take a look at what being a member of a radical team can mean in terms of both your professional development and your personal growth.

ARE RADICAL TEAMS FOR YOU?

Over and over again, people who have just completed their first radical team project ask the same questions:

- Why didn't someone warn me that the experience was going to be so intense, powerful, and, from time to time, frustratingly painful?
- Why wasn't I told that working on this project was going to be different from anything I have ever experienced before?
- Why didn't anyone explain that the project would stretch me professionally more than almost any other assignment in my career?

Surprisingly, people make such comments, even when they have been told exactly what to expect by others who have gone through the experience. Only by undergoing the process yourself will you be able to fully appreciate what they are talking about.

What makes the radical team experience so powerful? At the most basic level, the answer is human nature. We define ourselves by what we know and believe, by what we have accomplished in the past, and by our ability to enter unfamiliar situations with the confidence that we will be successful. Our accumulated knowledge and understandings constitute our personal identities. Our self-worth and credibility are rooted in the past. Yet increasingly we are being placed in situations in which our beliefs, knowledge, and expertise may no longer be applicable. Under these conditions the only wise thing to do is to admit ignorance. The only skill that is really important is the ability to learn.

Ultimately, learning is an existential act. It requires that we abandon old "truths" and long-held conceptions of the way the world works. It requires that we thoroughly and publicly embrace new and different views of reality. In response, a storm front of both passive and active resistance often settles in. Frustration, conflict, ambiguity, and tension are often at painful levels. To team members it sometimes feels as if full and irreconcilable breakdowns have occurred. Yet with some tolerance for ambiguity and some respect for each other, the storm passes. A world of new possibilities is suddenly opened up. New solutions become evident. This is what a real paradigm shift looks like. This is what it really means to break the frame. This is what it really takes to think out of the box.

Being a member of a radical team also challenges many of our traditional notions about teamwork and collaboration. It is not all hugs and warm fuzzies. As Peter Senge explains, "Contrary to popular myth, great teams are not characterized by an absence of conflict. On the contrary, in my experience, one of the most reliable indicators of a team that is continually learning is the visible conflict of ideas. In great teams, conflict becomes productive" (1990, p. 249). Cohesiveness and camaraderie are highly sought after in traditional teams. There is little acceptance of interpersonal conflict or impassioned emotions. Both are seen as potentially explosive and destructive. Radical teamwork is much messier. Emotions can run high. Differing perspectives are purposefully explored. Dissonance and creative tension form a backdrop that allows teams to challenge convention and explore possibilities that would otherwise be left untouched. Conformity and apathy are seen as the true dangers.

Not everyone is suited to be a member of a radical team. Certain people find the challenges and uncertainty exciting and motivational. Others find the same experiences discomforting and debilitating. What does it take to be a member of a radical team? It takes the willingness to tolerate high levels of ambiguity. It takes the strength to admit that you do not have the answers and do not know how to deal with the political realities that pervade your organization. It takes the courage to endure high levels of frustration. It takes the capacity to move beyond a prescribed functional role and adopt a broad, encompassing view of the business. It takes the ability to move out of your comfort zone and develop skills and capabilities you never thought you had.

The following profile (Figure 9.1) is based on the characteristics of those individuals who played critical roles in developing some of the most revolutionary new products in recent history. They also apply to the members of the radical teams described in this book. These individuals share four key characteristics: (1) they are challenge seekers; (2) they are continuous learners; (3) they are action- and results-driven; and (4) they align personal and organizational goals. Read the following characteristics and see how many apply to you. The more that apply, the more likely you will find the radical team process an exhilarating and positive experience.

Figure 9.1
Radical Team Member Profile

Challenge Seeker

1. I am quick to take on new challenges, even if I have not faced them before.
2. Above all else, I strive to make a difference in the company.
3. I challenge "the way it has been done before" as the only answer.
4. I try to tackle tough problems that nobody knows how to fix.
5. I create new opportunities when none exist.

Continuous Learner

1. I am a self-directed learner, continuously learning and changing as a result.
2. I possess strong curiosity, seeking out new ideas, perspectives, and opinions.
3. I use new ideas to solve problems.
4. I target learning to solve critical problems.
5. I listen carefully to new ideas and feedback.
6. I learn and adjust from feedback.

Action- or Results-Driven

1. I give top priority to getting results.
2. I convey a sense of urgency.
3. I persist in the face of obstacles, large or small.
4. I display a high level of energy.
5. I get things done.
6. I expect to succeed.

Goal-Oriented

1. I link personal and organizational goals into a unified goal.
2. I understand the direction and position of the business in the marketplace.
3. I build a strong connection between my own action and the organization's achieving its goals.
4. I display a strong personal commitment to the success of the business and to achieving my goals.
5. I accept total responsibility for the results.

Note: Adapted from Frohman, 1999. Used with permission.

RADICAL TEAMS AS CATALYSTS FOR PROFESSIONAL DEVELOPMENT

Many people turn back later in their careers and point to their involvement in radical teams as pivotal moments in their own professional development. Numerous studies have shown that the most successful executives, including many top CEOs, report that they developed key skills through stretch assignments and projects like those described in this book (McCauley, 1986). Radical team projects, by their nature, offer excellent opportunities for enhancing professional skills and knowledge. Because they require organizations to learn how to do something they cannot currently do, it is likely that they will also require the same of team members. Moreover, because radical teams gradually extend the breadth of their projects to include a wide range of organizational issues and factors, it is likely that team members will have the chance to develop knowledge and skills that are beyond their current areas of responsibility. Radical teams, as Glenn Parker (1994) points out, "provide an exciting opportunity for the creation of a learning community" (p. 137).

As I described earlier, some organizations seek to place an equal emphasis on projects and individual development by establishing structured action learning programs (Dotlich and Noel, 1998; Rothwell, 1999). However, the vast majority of projects are not incorporated within formal action learning programs. It is still possible for team members—either individually or in collaboration with others—to purposefully manage their projects as vehicles for professional development.

An obvious concern is that focusing on the professional development of team members might require extra time or reduce the quality of decisions. I am sure this happens in relatively rare cases. However, the evidence generally points in the opposite direction. Most teams report that a focus on professional development produces double-barreled pay offs. It helps people develop critical career competencies. It also generates better project results.

Here are some guidelines for building personal development into the radical team process.

Identify Personal Development Goals at the Beginning of Projects

A first step is to set your own professional development goals that relate to the project. You may have already established an overall set of development goals as part of a leadership development, management development, or career development program in your organization. You might have set some goals as part of your performance review process with your manager. Or you might just have identified some goals yourself on an informal basis.

Not all development goals can be met by all projects. However, it is highly likely that every radical project will provide the opportunity to work on one or more goals critical for your professional development. Here are examples of some goals that were set by members of radical teams at the beginning of their projects:

- Develop an ability to think outside the operational world, integrating marketing, financial, and technology perspectives.
- Learn the basics of financial analysis and cash flow.
- Understand the whole business, including business units and products that I know nothing about now.
- Develop the ability to lead a successful change effort, building support and overcoming resistance throughout the organization.
- Acquire the ability to analyze and take calculated risks.
- Enhance understanding of markets and customers.
- Start understanding the global side of the business.
- Develop the ability to rally the troops behind a revolutionary idea.
- Find out how to speed up the product development process.

Communicate Your Goals to Team Members

At the beginning of projects, it is important that team members understand each other's development goals and how members might be able to support each other in achieving these goals. Tell your teammates about your goals, and invite them to tell you about theirs as well. When doing so, be sure to tell others specifically what they can do to help you. This might include giving you feedback when you do or do not do certain things. It might include sharing their expertise and experience with you. It might involve negotiating to play certain roles in the project (such as facilitating team meetings to develop meeting leadership skills or making presentations to develop presentation skills). Obviously, you can provide the same help for your teammates. You need to serve as a mentor, coach, and supporter for your fellow team members, assisting them to achieve their professional development objectives at the same time you are working to achieve your own.

Periodically Stop and Review Progress on Development Goals

Suggest that your team stop at a few key points in the project to review progress being made on achieving professional development goals. This might initially sound hard to do, given the time constraints and the pressure for results. However, many teams are able to get into the habit of devoting some project time to discussing each person's professional development. If not, find ways to do so yourself. Stop and ask others for feedback on how well you are doing in achieving your goals. Take some time to reflect on how well you are doing in achieving your goals and what can be done through the remainder of your project to further develop desired skills and knowledge.

Keep a Record of Your Professional Development

Earlier I suggested that team members keep learning logs throughout their projects to record their perceptions of their projects from a team learning perspective. These same logs can be used to facilitate the achievement of professional development goals. Write your goals in the log. Record the steps you will take to achieve your goals. Stop and reflect on how well you are doing in achieving your goals.

Get Out of Your Comfort Zone

Try things you have not tried before. Go against the grain and do the opposite of what you might normally do. For example, I know of a team in which a marketing person and the finance person agreed to coach each other on each other's disciplines throughout a project, and whenever possible, to do project-related tasks that would most logically be assigned to the other person. As a result when the team presented its final recommendations to senior management, the finance person made a presentation on the marketing plans and vice versa, each person answering questions without the assistance of the other.

Work on Your Personal Learning Styles

Chapter Five discussed personal learning styles and team learning styles as they might be used to facilitate the overall team learning process. In addition, a focus on learning styles can help foster the professional development of team members. For example, someone who exhibits a very strong action-oriented style might set a goal to work on his or her reflection-oriented or planning-oriented style during the project. Then throughout the project other team members would provide feedback and coaching regarding the degree to which the person had exhibited this targeted learning style.

RADICAL TEAMS AS CATALYSTS FOR PERSONAL GROWTH

I am purposefully separating the topics of professional development and personal growth. Personal growth refers to how people are enriched in their understanding of themselves as individuals and in their relationships with others, apart from the professional skills and knowledge they might acquire at the same time.

When asked to look back over their careers and describe their peak work experiences, many people identify times when they were members of project teams working on particularly important and challenging tasks (Bennis and Biederman, 1997; Katzenbach and Smith, 1993). For many people, being a member of a radical team is a peak work experience that they will talk about for years to come. People look back and talk about their team experiences in almost spiritual terms. They are somehow transformed as individuals through their participation on certain teams.

The experience of working on radical teams provides a unique opportunity for personal growth. It strips away the superficiality of interpersonal relationships to get at core understandings. It provides a setting where people reveal themselves with candor and often make themselves vulnerable. It offers an environment that tests our abilities to be fully open to understanding other people who see the world differently and to grow from that experience.

Think back to your own peak work experiences: times you felt most fully engaged by compelling work that really made a difference; times that increased your self-awareness regarding personal motivations and your values; times that produced enduring personal relationships based on a respectful appreciation of others' differences. It is likely that one or more project team experiences will come to mind. I sincerely hope and expect that your future experiences applying the radical team approach in this book will produce memorable additions to your list of peak work experiences.

Above all else, this book is intended to serve as a practical, action-oriented handbook to an innovative approach to teamwork. It includes specific guidelines for action. It provides step-by-step exercises that can be immediately applied to teams. However, the real contribution of the book does not lie in specific techniques or methods. It is derived from deeper understandings of the underlying principles and a commitment to engaging yourself and your colleagues in the thoughtful application of these principles to the unique context of your projects. The exercises and techniques show one way to apply the approach. I am sure that you and your fellow team members will invent others that, based on the underlying principles, will allow you to be even more successful in your own situations.

Becoming skilled in the radical team approach takes continuing and persistent effort. I hope that you put the book in an easy-to-reach place on your bookshelf. I hope that each time you begin to work on a new project you pull it out and consider how you might further apply these principles and methods. I hope that you share the book with your fellow team members and explore how you might tackle your projects differently than you might have otherwise. I hope that the book, which is probably still in reasonably good physical condition, will soon be filled with dog-eared pages, scribbled notes, and coffee stains. Most important, I hope at some point in the future, at the end of a project that is critical to the success of your organization, you can look back and say to yourself, *"Our project made a real difference—to my organization, to my team, and to me."*

QUICK GUIDE TO APPLICATION EXERCISES

Team Application Exercise	Learning Dimension	Action Step	Page #	How to Use	When to Use		
					Early Project	Mid-Project	Late Project
5.1 Radical Project Checklist	Speed	1. Acknowledge uncertainty and the need to learn	85	Use to analyze new and potential projects to determine whether they are likely to require the radical team approach.	X		
5.2 Separating Assumptions from Facts	Speed	2. Separate facts from assumptions	90	Use at the beginning of projects to separate what teams actually know (facts) from what they think they know (assumptions).	X		
5.3 Team Learning Record	Speed	3. Act to learn	93	Use throughout projects to track "what we know," "what we don't know," and "what we assume." Then use it to design actions to increase learning and to record what has been learned as a result of the actions.	X	X	X
5.4 Keeping a Learning Cycle Record	Speed	4. Reduce learning cycle time	100	Use to track teams' learning cycles and plan for ways to reduce learning cycle time.		X	X
5.5 Learning Styles	Speed	5. Improve team learning	107	Use to help teams identify their most preferred and least preferred learning styles and plan actions to strengthen their least preferred styles.		X	X

6.1	Closer to Home	Depth	122	Use to help team members see the natural tendency to avoid solutions that require change on a personal level (best used after teams have had the chance to wrestle with their projects for a while).			X
6.2a	Personal Learning Log	Depth	123	Use to record team members' perceptions of projects—perceptions they may not have verbalized to colleagues. Teams can also use the logs during meetings to help open up and deepen team discussions.	X	X	X
6.2b	Ladder of Inference	Depth	125	Use to collectively sort through information teams gather and separate out objective data and concrete evidence from the interpretations and conclusions drawn from the evidence.		X	
6.3a	The TALK Model	Depth	127	Use to promote dialogue in team conversations in which there is a balance between advocacy and inquiry.	X	X	X
6.3b	A Recipe for More and Better Questions	Depth	130	Use to guide questioning when team members hold strongly held, differing opinions about their projects.	X	X	X

	Team Application Exercise	Learning Dimension	Action Step	Page #	How to Use	When to Use		
						Early Project	Mid-Project	Late Project
6.3c	Striking a Balance	Depth	3. Explore divergent views	130	Use to track the relative participation of team members and the degree to which team members tend to balance advocacy and inquiry.		X	
6.4	Reflecting on Roadblocks and Breakdowns	Depth	4. Use breakdowns to produce breakthroughs	136	Use to examine roadblocks and breakdowns as a means of producing project breakthroughs.		X	
6.5a	Capturing Lessons Learned	Depth	5. Capture lessons learned from cycle to cycle	139	Use to identify the lessons learned at the end of each learning cycle and explore their implications for projects.		X	X
6.5b	The Assumption-Learning Grid	Depth	5. Capture lessons learned from cycle to cycle	140	Use to summarize new information that has been gathered and determine if it supports previously defined assumptions.		X	X
6.6	Project Reframing Grid	Depth	6. Reframe the project	143	Use to guide teams in reframing their projects.		X	X
7.1a	Creating a Domain Map	Breadth	1. Uncover connections	155	Use at the beginning of projects to identify potential forces and factors that teams should investigate.	X		

	Name	Category	Subcategory	Page	Description			
7.1b	Using the Narrow-to-Broad Continuum	Breadth	1. Uncover connections	157	Use during projects to help teams consider the need to broaden the scope of their projects.	X		
7.1c	Reverse Flow Chart	Breadth	1. Uncover connections	159	Use toward the end of projects to summarize complex cause-and-effect relationships that teams have discovered.			X
7.2	Identifying the Key Players	Breadth	2. Reach out to influence others	162	Use to identify project stake-holders and guide teams in developing proactive strategies for managing their influences on projects.		X	
7.3a	Learning from Past Projects	Breadth	3. Learn from the past	166	Use to systematically analyze past projects that have the potential to influence current projects.		X	
7.3b	Creating a Time Line	Breadth	3. Learn from the past	167	Use to create a historical time line of events and forces related to projects.		X	
7.4	Challenging the Culture	Breadth	4. Go against the organizational grain	172	Use to develop countercultural team norms as needed to achieve desired project outcomes.	X	X	
7.5	Creating an Impact Plan	Breadth	5. Make things happen elsewhere	175	Use to plan how the team will maximize the influence of its project on the entire organization.			X

NOTES

Chapter One

1. The quotation is taken from a speech given by Angela Davis entitled "Let Us All Rise Together," given at Spelman College, June 25, 1987. It is reprinted in her book *Women, Culture, and Politics* (New York: Random House, 1989).
2. Collaborators in conducting the team learning studies included Laurel Jeris, Richard Kamm, Judy O'Neil, Michael Moran, Jeanne Connolly, Sarah May, Eric McLaren, Ellen McMahon, John Niemi, and Ralph Catalanello. More specific descriptions of the contribution of individuals are presented in the notes to Chapter Four.
3. Ralph Catalanello and I originated the concepts of speed, depth, and breadth in the book *Strategic Readiness: The Making of the Learning Organization* (San Francisco: Jossey-Bass, 1994). In *Strategic Readiness,* the terms were applied to the strategic planning process of organizations rather than team projects.

Chapter Two

1. A listing of terms used is provided at the end of this book that defines terms that are likely to be unfamiliar, such as *Gantt charts* and *critical path method.* Look at the following excellent sources for more information on commonly accepted processes and techniques of project management: *A Guide to the Project Management Body of Knowledge* (1998), *The Field Guide to Project Management* (Cleland, 1998*), The New Project Management* (Frame, 1994), and *The Project Management Institute: Project Management Handbook* (Pinto, 1998).

Chapter Three

1. The research team for comparison group 1 consisted of several graduate students at Northern Illinois University, including Laurel Jeris, Michael Moran, Eric McLaren, Sarah May, Jeanne Connolly, Ellen McMahon, and Lucille Coleman. In addition, professors John Niemi and Ralph Catalanello provided valuable assistance in designing the study.

More information about the study can be found as follows: "Team Learning Processes, Interventions, and Assessments" (Jeris, May, and Redding, 1997); "Team Learning Consultation: Pilot Study of an Alternative to Process Consultation" (Redding, Jeris, Connolly, and Moran, 1997).

2. This group was studied as part of an evaluation project completed by the Institute for Strategic Learning for an action learning program conducted for Partners for the Learning Organization consulting group in a large public utility. Thanks go to Judy O'Neill of Partners for the Learning Organization and to Laurel Jeris for their participation and support of this study.

3. Comparison group 3 was studied as part of an Institute for Strategic Learning consulting assignment. Thanks go to Richard Kamm, former education director, the Ball Foundation.

4. Comparison group 4 was studied as part of an Institute for Strategic Learning consulting assignment.

5. Comparison group 5 was studied as part of an Institute for Strategic Learning consulting assignment.

Chapter Five

1. This interview is reported by Amy Edmonson, "Psychological Safety and Learning Behavior in Work Teams," *Administrative Science Quarterly,* 1999, *44*(2), p. 374.

2. I am unsure where and when I first came across the Checking Your Baggage exercise. I began using it with teams of teachers to help teams approach their projects without preconceived solutions, or at least to hold preconceived ideas more lightly.

3. Michael Pacanowsky describes color questioning in "Team Tools for Wicked Problems," *Organizational Dynamics,* 1995, *23*(3), p. 41.

4. I adapted this exercise from a technique I learned from Mark Cheren of Strategic Learning Services, which, in turn, was based on problem-based learning methods used to train physicians (Barrows, 1985).

5. The story of Team New Zealand is from K. Maani and C. Benton, "Rapid Team Learning: Lessons from Team New Zealand America's Cup Campaign," *Organizational Dynamics,* 1999, *27*(4), 48–62.

6. A great deal has been written on the idea of personal learning styles, as opposed to team learning styles. For example, both David Kolb (1984) and Peter Honey and Alan Mumford (1995a) identify specific learning styles that link to each stage of the learning cycle. I have adapted this same approach for use in identifying the collective learning styles of teams as a whole. I am especially indebted to Honey and Mumford's learning styles approach (1995a, 1995b).

Chapter Six

1. The description of the Cochlear Implant Project is derived from R. Garud and A. H. Van de Ven, "An Empirical Evaluation of the Internal Corporate Venturing Process," *Strategic Management Journal,* 1992, *13,* 93–109.

2. Thanks go to Laurel Jeris for introducing me to the "Closer to Home" exercise.
3. The ladder of inference is a somewhat simplified version of the one outlined by Chris Argyris in *Knowledge for Action* (San Francisco: Jossey-Bass, 1993).

Chapter Seven
1. More detail on systems archetypes can be found in Peter Senge and associates' book, *The Fifth Discipline Fieldbook* (New York: Doubleday, 1994).

Chapter Eight
1. This quote by Edgar Schein is from his article "How Can Organizations Learn Faster? The Challenge of Entering the Green Room." *Sloan Management Review,* 1993, *35* (Winter), p. 90.
2. Information on the U.S. Army's use of after action review (AAR), as well as its application to business organizations, comes from L. Baird, P. Holland, and S. Deacon, "Learning from Action: Imbedding More Learning into Performance Fast Enough to Make a Difference," *Organizational Dynamics,* 1999, *27*(4), 19–32. Copies of the army's training manual, *A Leader's Guide to After-Action Reviews* (TC-25–20), can be obtained through the Center for Army Lessons Learned (CALL) website: [http://call.armymil.call.html]. A videotape highlighting the AAR process called *Mohavia: In Pursuit of Agility* is available from MGA Media, 200 West 60th St., #31F, New York, NY 10023.
3. The Ernst & Young study described here was reported in a presentation by Nancy Dixon and Jonathan Ungerleider, "How to Build, Support, and Maintain a Viable Lessons Learned Initiative," at the 1997 Knowledge Management Conference, San Diego, California, December 1997.

TERMS USED IN THIS BOOK

Action learning: A form of leadership development that uses real-world problems and projects as vehicles for professional growth and development.

Action science: A methodology developed by Chris Argyris and Donald Schön, designed to increase double-loop learning. According to Argyris and Schön (1996), action science creates "conditions for collaborative inquiry in which people . . . function as co-researchers . . . making private attributions public, treating these attributions as disconfirmable, and subjecting them to public test" (p. 50).

Assumption: A premise—either unstated or stated—that has not been explicitly verified by objective evidence.

Breadth: One of three dimensions of team learning that form the basis of the radical team approach as described in this book (along with speed and depth). Breadth refers to the degree to which teams have an impact on their organizations as whole systems, often affecting issues critical to the strategic success of the enterprise.

Champions (project champions): Usually senior-level managers within the business units or divisions in which project teams operate. Champions are often the first to propose projects and usually serve as the primary advocates for projects from beginning to end. In some cases groups collectively serve as champions (such as senior management teams and other committees). In some organizations and with some project teams, champions are formally designated. Other times, people serve informally in this role.

Critical path (critical path method): A project management technique that begins by using flow charting to map out the interrelationships of steps in a complex project. Each step is assigned an amount of time that is required to complete the step. A "critical path" is then identified, consisting of a series of interrelated steps that take the longest time to complete. The management of the project then focuses on ensuring that all steps in the critical path are completed on or before schedule.

Depth: One of three dimensions of team learning that form the basis of the radical team approach as described in this book (along with speed and breadth). Depth refers to the degree to which teams deepen their understanding of problems rather than accept the way tasks might initially appear; when appropriate, teams develop solutions based on framing assumptions that are different from those that existed at the beginning of the projects. Using Argyris and Schön's (1996) terminology, depth refers to the degree to which teams engage in double-loop learning (see "Double-loop learning"). Radical teams reframe their problems as they work through projects.

Dialogue: A conversation between two or more people characterized by a balance between advocacy and inquiry. According to Peter Senge (1990), most team conversations consist of the one-sided advocacy of the individual positions held by team members. As in ping-pong matches, the ball is hit back and forth over the net, and there are often winners and losers. In contrast, dialogue refers to a different form of conversation that occurs when team members take special care to balance advocacy (presenting one's own opinions) with inquiry (openly seeking to be influenced by others). When engaging in dialogue, team members suspend their own beliefs and assumptions to the degree possible and engage each other in a collaborative pursuit of new meaning.

Double-loop learning: One of two forms of organizational learning, according to Chris Argyris and Donald Schön (1996). One form, single-loop learning, occurs without changing framing assumptions (see "Framing assumptions"). The other form, double-loop learning, occurs by changing the framing assumptions. "Single-loop learning is appropriate for the routine, repetitive issues—it helps get the everyday job done. Double-loop learning is more relevant for the complex, nonprogrammable issues—it assures that there will be another day in the future of the organization" (Argyris, 1992, p. 9). Throughout the book, the term reframing (see "Reframing") is used as a rough equivalent to double-loop learning.

Framing: "The process by which we define the decision to be made, the ends to be achieved, the means which may be chosen" (Schön, 1983, p. 40). Schön continues: "In real-world practice, problems do not present themselves to the practitioner as givens. They must be constructed from the materials of problematic situations which are puzzling, troubling, and uncertain. In order to convert a problematic situation to a problem, a practitioner must do a certain kind of work. He must make sense of an uncertain situation that initially makes no sense."

Framing assumption: An assumption (see "Assumption"), usually unstated, that determines the way projects are defined and approached by an organization or team.

Gantt chart: A commonly used technique for scheduling a complex project. It consists of defining the tasks and subtasks of a project and visually showing their sequencing on a time line. As with the critical path method (see "Critical path"), the Gantt chart represents a primarily linear (rather than a learning cycle) approach to project management.

Learning cycle: The idea that learning, whether by individuals or teams, can be understood as an iterative process consisting of a repeating series of defined steps. The team learning cycle described in this book has four steps: (1) Understand and Frame the Project, (2) Plan, (3) Act, and (4) Reflect and Learn. Any project can be understood as a series of repeating learning cycles.

Learning cycle time: The total length of time needed to complete a team learning cycle. Not to be confused with project cycle time (see "Project cycle time").

Learning style: The degree to which individuals or teams have preferences for one or more steps in the learning cycle over others (see "Team learning style").

Project management: Any methodology for defining, planning, reviewing, and evaluating projects. Most traditional methods of project management are based on a linear, sequential approach to looking at projects (see "Critical path," "Gantt chart," "Stage-gate process," and "waterfall model"). In contrast, a team learning approach to project management is rooted in seeing projects as an iterative, nonlinear discovery process (see "Team learning cycle").

Project Management Body of Knowledge (PMBOK): The commonly accepted project management practices as defined by the Project Management Institute—the leading international project management professional association. PMBOK is described in "A Guide to the Project Management Body of Knowledge," which is available on the Project Management Institute's website (www.pmi.org).

Project cycle time: Total time from the beginning to end of a project—not to be confused with learning cycle time.

Radical teams: Teams that achieve breakthrough results by harnessing the power of team learning. Radical teams are identified by comparing the speed, depth, and breadth of their learning to that of comparable teams (see "Speed," "Depth," and "Breadth").

Rapid applications development: A method of software development that uses an iterative, team learning process to dramatically decrease total project cycle time (Martin, 1989a, 1989b).

Reframing: The process through which teams discard initial framing assumptions and approach their projects from a different set of framing assumptions. Throughout this book reframing is used as shorthand for double-loop learning (see "Double-loop learning").

Single-loop learning: See "Double-loop learning."

Speed: One of three dimensions of team learning that form the basis of the radical team approach as described in this book (along with depth and breadth). Speed refers to learning cycle time, or the number of learning cycles completed over a given time. Radical teams usually complete more learning cycles over a given period of time than comparable teams.

Sponsors (project sponsors): Generally, mid-level or senior managers who possess management responsibilities for areas most directly related to specific projects. Their job is to work directly with project teams, providing whatever support is needed during projects. They are the first persons teams turn to when problems and issues arise during projects. In some organizations and with some project teams, sponsors are formally designated. Other times, people serve in this role informally.

Stage-gate process: A project control method that consists of establishing predetermined checkpoints between stages of a project. In most cases, stage-gate reviews consist of project teams presenting progress on their projects to a review body (often made up of senior management) that uses preestablished criteria to determine whether to give a go-ahead to move to the next stage.

Team learning cycle: The use of the learning cycle as the primary unit of analysis to portray what occurs over the course of team-based projects. The team learning cycle described in this book has four steps: (1) Understand and Frame the Project, (2) Plan, (3) Act, and (4) Reflect and Learn. Any project can be understood as a series of repeating learning cycles.

Team learning style: The learning style (see "Learning style"), as represented by the collective actions of a team.

Waterfall model: The traditional model of the life cycle of a project. A project is seen as a series of sequential, nonoverlapping stages in which each stage creates the product that initiates the next stage. One stage of the project is not started until the next stage is complete. Often there are standard review processes (see "Stage-gate process") that occur between stages.

REFERENCES

Argyris, C. *On Organizational Learning.* Cambridge, Mass.: Blackwell, 1992.

Argyris, C. *Knowledge for Action.* San Francisco: Jossey-Bass, 1993.

Argyris C., and Schön, D. *Organizational Learning II.* Reading, Mass.: Addison-Wesley, 1996.

Baird, L., Holland, P., and Deacon, S. "Learning from Action: Imbedding More Learning into Performance Fast Enough to Make a Difference." *Organizational Dynamics,* 1999, *27*(4), 19–32.

Barrows, J. S. *How to Design a Problem-Based Curriculum for the Preclinical Years.* New York: Springer, 1985.

Bennis, W., and Biederman, P. W. *Organizing Genius.* Reading, Mass.: Addison-Wesley, 1997.

Cleland, D. *Field Guide to Project Management.* New York: Wiley, 1998.

Davis, A. *Women, Culture, and Politics.* New York: Random House, 1989.

Dewey, J. *Logic: The Theory of Inquiry.* New York: Holt, Rinehart and Winston, 1938.

Dixon, N. *The Organizational Learning Cycle.* London: McGraw-Hill, 1994.

Dotlich, D. L., and Noel, J. L. *Action Learning.* San Francisco: Jossey-Bass, 1998.

Edmondson, A. "Psychological Safety and Learning Behavior in Work Teams." *Administrative Science Quarterly,* 1999, *44*(2), 350–383.

Eisenhardt, K., and Tabrizi, B. N. "Accelerating Adaptive Processes: Product Innovation in the Global Computer Industry." *Administrative Science Quarterly,* 1995, *40*(1), 84–111.

Frame, J. D. *The New Project Management.* San Francisco: Jossey-Bass, 1994.

Frohman, A. L. "Personal Initiative Sparks Innovation." *Research and Technology Management,* 1999, *42*(3), 32–38.

Garud, R., and Van de Ven, A. H. "An Empirical Evaluation of the Internal Corporate Venturing Process." *Strategic Management Journal,* 1992, *13*, 93–109.

A Guide to the Project Management Body of Knowledge. New Town Square, Penn.: Project Management Institute, 1998.

Honey, P., and Mumford, A. *Capitalizing on Your Learning Style.* King of Prussia, Penn.: HRDQ, 1995a.

Honey, P., and Mumford A. *Learning Styles Questionnaire.* King of Prussia, Penn.: HRDQ, 1995b.

Janis, I. L. *Groupthink: Psychological Studies of Policy Decisions and Fiascoes.* Boston: Houghton-Mifflin, 1982.

Jeris, L. "An Empirical Study of the Relationship Between Team Process Interventions and Double-loop Learning." Unpublished doctoral dissertation, Department of Leadership and Educational Policy Studies, Northern Illinois University, 1997.

Jeris, L., May, S., and Redding J. "Team Learning Processes, Interventions and Assessments." *Organization Development Journal,* 1997, *15*(1), 92–99.

Juran, J. M. *Juran on Planning for Quality.* New York: The Free Press, 1988.

Katzenbach, J. R., and Smith, D. K. *The Wisdom of Teams.* Boston: Harvard Business School Press, 1993.

Kolb, D. *Experiential Learning.* Upper Saddle River, N.J.: Prentice Hall, 1984.

Kotnour, T. "A Learning Framework for Project Management." *Project Management Journal,* 1999, *30*(2), 32–38.

Kuhn, T. *The Structure of Scientific Revolutions.* Chicago, Ill.: University of Chicago Press, 1970.

Lewin, K. *Field Theory in Social Science.* New York: HarperCollins, 1951.

Lynn, G. S., Mazzuca, M., Morone, J. G., and Paulson, A. S. "Learning Is the Most Critical Thing in Developing Really New Products." *Research and Technology Management,* 1998, *41*(3), 45–51.

Maani, K., and Benton, C. "Rapid Team Learning: Lessons from Team New Zealand America's Cup Campaign." *Organizational Dynamics,* 1999, *27*(4), 48–62.

Martin, J. "RAD Designed to Facilitate Dynamic Change in Firms. *PC Week,* 1989a, *6*(50), 64.

Martin, J. "RAD Techniques Are a Must for Retooling the IS Factory." *PC Week,* 1989b, *6*(51), 52.

McCauley, C. D. *Development Experiences in Managerial Work.* Technical Report Number 26. Greensboro, N.C.: Center for Creative Leadership, 1986.

Pacanowsky, M. "Team Tools for Wicked Problems." *Organizational Dynamics,* 1995, *23*(3), 36–51.

Parker, G. M. *Cross-Functional Teams.* San Francisco: Jossey-Bass, 1994.

Pascale, R. T., and Miller, A. H. "The Action Lab: Creating a Greenhouse for Organizational Change." *Strategy & Business,* 1999, *17*(4), 64–74.

Pinto, J. (ed.). *The Project Management Institute: Project Management Handbook.* San Francisco: Jossey-Bass, 1998.

Redding, J., and Catalanello, R. *Strategic Readiness: The Making of the Learning Organization.* San Francisco: Jossey-Bass, 1994.

Redding, J., Jeris, L., Connolly, J., and Moran, N. "Team Learning Consultation: Pilot Study of an Alternative to Process Consultation." In E. F. Holton III (ed.), *Academy of Human Resource Development Proceedings.* Austin, Tex.: Academy of Human Resource Development, 1997, pp. 139–144.

Revans, R. W. *The Origins and Growth of Action Learning.* Chartwell/Brant, U.K.: Bromley, 1982.

Rice, M. P., O'Connor, G. C., Peters, L. S., and Morone, J. G. "Managing Discontinuous Innovation." *Research-Technology Management,* 1998, *41*(3), 52–58.

Rothwell, W. *The Action Learning Guidebook.* San Francisco: Jossey-Bass, 1999.

Schein, E. H. "How Can Organizations Learn Faster? The Challenge of Entering the Green Room." *Sloan Management Review,* 1993, *35*(Winter), 85–92.

Schein, E. J. "The Role of Leadership in the Management of Organizational Transformation and Learning." *OD Practitioner,* 1999, *27*(1), 17–24.

Schön, D. *The Reflective Practitioner: How Professionals Think in Action.* New York: Basic Books, 1983.

Senge, P. *The Fifth Discipline.* New York: Doubleday, 1990.

Senge, P., and Associates. *The Fifth Discipline Fieldbook.* New York: Doubleday, 1994.

Tate, P. "Shooting the Application Development Rapids." *PC Week,* 1998, *15*(21), 97.

Vesey, J. T. "The New Competitors: They Think in Terms of Speed to Market." *Academy of Management Executive,* 1991, *5*(2), 23–33.

Watkins, K., and Marsick, V. *Sculpting the Learning Organization.* San Francisco: Jossey-Bass, 1993.

Weick, K. *The Social Psychology of Organizing.* Reading, Mass.: Addison-Wesley, 1979.

Wycloff, J. *Mindmapping.* New York: Berkley Press, 1991.

INDEX

Past projects, learning from, 71–72, 164–168; examples of, 165; exercises for, 165–168, 213

Paulson, A. S., 29

Peak work experiences, 206

Peers of project team members, 161

Performance Management Team: profile of, 14; team learning of, assessed, 51

Permission seeking, 72, 171

Personal experience of radical team members, 199–203

Personal growth, radical teams as catalysts for, 205–206. *See also* Professional development

Personal learning logs, 114–115, 123–124; exercise for, 123–124, 211; in project team research study, 114–115, 126–127, 133; for tracking professional development, 205

Personal learning styles, 106; working on, 205–206

Personal stakes: of stakeholders, 163–164; of team members, 122, 190

Peters, L. S., 11

Plan execution, acting to learn versus, 63

Planning: action and, 63; learning style associated with, 104; for reducing project time, 94; in team learning cycle, 32–33

Planning-oriented teams, 104

Politics, 175, 184

Postmortems, 30, 174–175

Preconceived solutions, avoiding, 86–87

Presentations, 173–174, 194

Privacy, norm of, 119

Problem-solving exercises, traditional versus alternative approaches to, 8–10

Problems. *See* Projects

Process issues, organizational, 155

Product innovation, 11–12; case example of, 186–187; learning-based approach to, 29; learning versus project cycle time and, 94–95; skunk works methods of, 99

Production Scheduling Team: customer partnerships of, 152–153; domain map of, 149–151, 152; executive committee and, 151, 152, 181, 183; leadership support for, 181, 183; learning cycles of, 149–153; profile of, 14; project of, 148–149; as radical team, 16, 54, 60; results

of, 19, 153; stakeholder involvement of, 151, 152–153, 154; story of, 148–153; team learning of, assessed, 54, 55

Professional development, 203–206; goals for, communicating to team members, 204; goals for, examples of, 204; goals for, identifying, 203–204; personal learning styles and, 205–206; recordkeeping of, 205; review of, 205; for stakeholders, 164; for team members, 191, 203–206

Project champions. *See* Champions

Project cycle time, 64; defined, 95, 222; learning cycle time versus, 64, 94–95; reducing, 94–95

Project definition: breadth of, 147–176; complex cause-effect relationships and, 158–161; domain mapping for, 155–156, 159; end results and, 188–189; guidelines for, 187–189; leadership support for, 187–189; learning and, 27–30; learning style associated with, 103–104; narrow-to-broad continuum of, 156–158; reframing, 141–145; in team learning cycle, 31–32, 33; traditional versus radical approach to, 28, 30, 69–70; tunnel vision in, 69–70; uncovering connections in, 69–70, 154–161. *See also* Breadth; Framing; Reframing; Scope

Project management, 220, 221; defined, 221; training in, 194

Project management body of knowledge (PMBOK), 222

Project Management Institute, 222

Project postmortems, 30, 174–175

Project Reframing Grid, 143–145, 212

Project reporting: guidelines for, 173–174; premature, 171

Project sponsors. *See* Sponsors

Project team study: comparison groups in, 49–57, 59–60; evaluation of team learning in, 13, 15–18, 39–57; methodologies of, 13, 49–50, 59–60, 114; overview of, 13–19; projects of, characteristics of, 49; radical teams in, action steps of, listed, 17–18; radical teams in, listed, 16; radical teams in, results of, 18–19; radical-traditional comparison groups in, 59–60; team learning practices in, 59–74; team profiles in, 14. *See also* Radical teams

Project teams: assessment of, 39–57; projects of, examples of, 3–5; in research study, listed, 14; traditional versus alternative, in examples, 5–10; traditional versus radical, in team learning, 59–74; traditional versus radical, results of, 18–19. *See also* Radical teams; Traditional teams

Projects: assessment of, for uncertainty, 84–87; breadth dimension of, 16, 40, 147–176; criteria for, that require radical teams, 11–13, 84, 188; depth dimension of, 15–16, 40, 111–145; framing and reframing, 9–10, 15–17, 68; framing and reframing, in Order Cancellation Team example, 23–26, 33; framing and reframing, in team learning cycle, 31–32, 33, 34; learning-based approach to, 27–30; mission-critical, examples of, 3–5; past, learning from, 71–72, 164–168, 213; radical team results for, 18–19; of research study project teams, 14, 49; selection of, 187–188; speed dimension of, 13, 39, 60–65, 77–110; team learning styles and, 105–106; traditional approaches to, 28, 30; uncertainty in, 83–87; wicked versus tame, 11–13

Provocative questions, 130

Public school project teams, listed, 14. *See also* Mathematics Improvement Team; Parent Involvement Team; Reading Improvement Team; Writing Improvement Team

Public utilities. *See* Utility organizations

Publishing company, 22; customer service problem of, 4; project team of, 14, 22–26. *See also* Order Cancellation Team

Purpose statement, 189

Q

Questions: balancing advocacy with, 130–132; detail, 130; exercise for posing, 130, 211; exercises for, 129–132; exploring divergent views and, 126–132; open-ended, 130; provocative, 130; for reframing, 142, 143–144; safe environment for, 115–122; summary, 130; team members' reluctance to voice, 114–115, 133–134; techniques for posing, 87, 129–130. *See also* Inquiry

R

Radar, flying under the, 171

Radical, defined, 10–11

Radical innovations, 11–12

Radical Project Checklist, 85, 210

Radical teams: action steps of, listed, 17–18; breadth in, action steps to increase, 147–176; breadth in, versus in traditional teams, 61, 69–73; defined, 222; depth in, action steps to increase, 111–145; depth in, versus in traditional teams, 61, 65–68; ground rules for, 102, 103, 119–121; key differences between traditional teams and, 61; learning approach of, 27–30; listed, 14, 16, 60; meetings of, 6–8; member profile for, 201–202; mini-cultures of, 170–172; origins of concept, 5–18; personal side of, 199–207; practices of, listed, 61; problems that require, criteria for, 11–13, 84, 188; professional development in, 203–206; results of, versus traditional teams, 18–19; speed in, actions steps to increase, 77–110; speed in, versus in traditional teams, 60–65; support for, 177–197; team learning of, versus comparison teams, 50–57; team learning of, versus traditional teams, 28, 30, 59–74; traditional teams versus, 5–10, 59–74, 103, 201. *See also* Cost Reduction Team; Mathematics Improvement Team; North American Consolidation—Marketing Team; Order Cancellation Team; Production Scheduling Team

Rapid applications development (RAD), 29, 222

Reading Improvement Team: profile of, 14; team learning of, assessed, 53; as traditional team example, 60

Recipe for More and Better Questions, 130, 211

Recognition, for stakeholders, 164, 173

Redding, J., 31

Reducing Duplicate Operations Team: profile of, 14; team learning of, assessed, 52

Reflecting on Roadblocks and Breakdowns, 136–137, 212

Reflection: for capturing lessons learned, 139; learning style associated with, 105; on roadblocks and breakdowns, 136–137; in team learning cycle, 32, 33, 35

Reflection-oriented teams, 105
Reframing, 141–145; breakdowns and, 67–68; collective, 142; containing versus, 68; defined, 222; depth and, 15–16, 115, 141–145; double-loop learning and, 220, 222; examples of, 141–142; exercise for, 143–145, 212; experimental research on, 9–10; multiple learning cycles and, 142; obstacles to, 114–115; in Order Cancellation Team example, 23–26, 33, 34, 141, 142; preparing stakeholders for, 71; questions for, 142, 143–144. *See also* Assumptions; Framing
Resistance: organizational culture and, 168–174; of stakeholders, 71, 163–164, 175; techniques for minimizing, 163–164, 170–172, 175
Resources, in Project Reframing Grid, 144
Restructuring Team: failure of, to learn from conflict, 133–136; failure of, to reframe project, 141–142; profile of, 14; project of, 133; story of, 133–135; team learning of, assessed, 51; as traditional team example, 60
Results: project definition in terms of, 188–189; of radical teams, summarized, 18–19
Revans, R. W., 162
Reverse flow chart, 159–161; exercise for creating, 159–161, 213; sample, 160
Rice, M. P., 11
Risk-related assumptions, 120–122
Risk taking: culture and, 72–73, 168; gradual approach to, 121; safe environment for, 115–122; safety versus, 66
Road map, 28
Roadblocks. *See* Breakdowns; Conflict
Role models, leaders as, 183–184
Root, radical and, 10–11
Ross, R., 128–129
Rothwell, W., 203

S

Safety: areas requiring, 116; for depth of learning, 115–122; exercise for, 122, 211; external factors in, 117, 182–183; focus on, versus risk, 66; guidelines for establishing, 119–121; leadership support for, 182–183; in Mathematics Improvement Team example, 116–119

Schein, E. J., 115, 177
Schön, D., 9, 10, 116, 219, 220, 221
Scope: breadth of learning and, 147–176; complex cause-effect relationships and, 158–161; domain mapping of, 155–156, 159; narrow-to-broad continuum of, 156–158; systemic approach and, 37–38, 48, 69–70, 147–148, 173–176; traditional versus radical approach to, 28, 69–73; uncovering connections in, 154–161. *See also* Breadth; Project definition
Sculpting the Learning Organization (Watkins and Marsick), 127–128
Searle, 29
Selection: of projects, 187–188; of team members, 185–186, 189–191
Self-esteem, stakeholder, 164
Senge, P., 88, 127, 129, 153–154, 159, 201, 220
Senior executives, 161, 163. *See also* Leadership support
Sense of urgency, 182
Separating Assumptions from Facts exercise, 90, 210
Sharing: of credit, 174, 175; of learning, 174–175
Shifting the Burden archetype, 159
Simulations, 95, 187
Single-loop learning, 220
Skills, team member, 191
Skunk works, 99
Small medical products manufacturer, 186–187
Smith, D. K., 206
Socrates, 83
Soft support, 178–184; defined, 177; examples of, 179–181; guidelines for, 182–184; leadership roles for, 178–179. *See also* Leadership support; Support
Software application development, 29, 222
Speed, 77–110; action step 1 (acknowledge uncertainty and need to learn) for, 83–87, 210; action step 2 (separate assumptions from facts) for, 87–91, 210; action step 3 (act to learn) for, 91–94, 210; action step 4 (reduce learning cycle time) for, 94–101, 210; action step 5 (improve the learning process), 102–109; action steps for, 17, 74, 77–78, 83–110; action

steps for, listed, 77–78; assumptions versus facts and, 87–91; Cost Reduction Team example of, 78–81; defined, 13, 77, 222; evaluation of, 13, 39, 44, 47; evaluation of, for research study comparison groups, 50–57; exercises for increasing, 85–87, 89–90, 92–94, 97–98, 100–101, 106–109, 210–211; learning cycle time and, 94–101; learning process and, 102–109; measurement of, 13, 44, 47; practices of, listed, 61; in radical versus traditional teams, 60–65; uncertainty and, 62, 83–87

Sponsor(s): of Cost Reduction Team, 80; defined, 179, 222–223; examples of, 179–181; of Order Cancellation Team, 179–180; political expertise of, 175, 184; preparing, for project reframing, 71; as stakeholders, 161. *See also* Leadership support

Staff Empowerment Team: profile of, 14; team learning of, assessed, 52

Stage-gate process, 28, 64, 223

Stakeholders: defined, 161; exercise for identifying, 162–163, 213; formal roles for, 164; identifying, 162–163, 213; influencing, strategies for, 70–71, 161–164, 213; influencing, versus being influenced by, 70–71, 162; involving, for breadth, 154, 175; limiting the influence of, 170–171; obtaining support of, 163–164; personal priorities of, 163–164; reframing and, 143; resistance of, 71, 163–164, 175; types of, 161

Stand-up meetings, 99

Status quo, 89, 182

Strategic planning, 31, 186–187

Streamline Operations Team, 53

Striking a Balance exercise, 130–132, 212

Structures and systems, support from, 177, 185–187

Subject matter experts, 161, 179

Summary information, 99–100

Summary questions, 130

Suppliers, as stakeholders, 161

Supply chain issues, 154

Support, 177–197; categories of, 177–178; guidelines for, 187–197; hard, 177–178, 185–187; obtaining stakeholders', 163–164, 175; soft, 177, 178–184

Symbolic actions, countercultural, 73

System archetypes, 159

Systems approach: breadth and, 69, 147–176; learning and, 27, 48; project definition and, 37–38, 69–70; taking responsibility for impact and, 73, 175

Systems thinking, 152–153

T

Tabrizi, B. N., 29, 95

TALK model, 127–128, 211

Talking, 126–132. *See also* Dialogue

Tate, P., 29

Team charters, 143, 185

Team composition: assumptions and, 88–89; team members selection and, 189–191

Team dynamics, 64–65

Team ground rules, 102, 103

Team leaders, 179

Team learning: action for, 91–94; assessment of, 13, 15–18, 39–57; capturing, from cycle to cycle, 68, 138–141; in comparison group 1, 50, 51; in comparison group 2, 50, 52; in comparison group 3, 53, 54; in comparison group 4, 54, 55; in comparison group 5, 54, 56; from conflict, 67–68, 132–137; focus on team dynamics versus, 64–65; improving, approaches to, 102–109; learning styles and, 102–109; practices of, listed, 61; in radical teams versus traditional teams, 59–74; role models for, 183–184; sharing, with organization, 174–175; tracking, 197. *See also* Breadth; Capturing lessons learned; Depth; Evaluation of breadth; Evaluation of depth; Evaluation of speed; Evaluation of team learning; Learning; Lessons learned; Speed

Team learning cycle map(s), 34; for Cost Reduction Team, 82; for Order Cancellation Team, 36

Team learning cycle(s), 13; assumptions throughout multiple, 90–91; awareness of, building, 96–98; capturing lessons learned at end of each, 68, 138–141; defined, 223; learning styles and, 102–109; in Mathematics Improvement Team example, 117–118; meetings and, 96–97; in Order Cancellation Team example, 33–38;

overview of, 30–33; process of, 32–33; reducing time of, 64, 94–101; reframing throughout multiple, 142; speed of, 44, 47, 63, 81–83; speed of, techniques for increasing, 95–101; step 1 (understand and frame the project) in, 31–32, 33, 34; step 2 (plan) in, 32–33; step 3 (act) in, 32, 33, 35; step 4 (reflect and learn) in, 32, 33, 35; steps of, 31–33. *See also* Learning cycle time

Team Learning Record, 92–94, 210

Team learning styles, 102–109; action-oriented, 104–105; defined, 223; exercise regarding, 106–109, 210; framing-oriented, 103–104; graphic illustration of, 104; guidelines for identifying, 106–109; guidelines for improving, 105–106; planning-oriented, 104; reflection-oriented, 105

Team members: characteristics of radical teams and, 199–202; communicating personal goals to, 204; personal experience of, 199–203; personal growth of, 206–207; professional development of, 203–206; profile of, 201–202; selection of, 185–186, 189–191

Team New Zealand, 95–96

Team norms, 119–121, 171–172

Team performance, impact of learning on, 29

Teamwork: experimental research study on, 8–10; traditional versus alternative, 5–10; traditional versus radical, 59–74. *See also* Radical teams

Technology issues, 154

Tension. *See* Breakdowns; Conflict

"Think out of the box" lecture, 182–183

Time line: current project, 145; historical, 167–168, 213

Tracking, 197, 205

Traditional teams and teamwork: alternative teamwork versus, 5–10; approaches of, to projects, 28, 30, 64; breadth in, versus in radical teams, 61, 69–73; comparison groups of, 59–60; conflict and, 133–136, 201; depth in, versus in radical teams, 61, 65–68; experimental research study on, 8–10; ground rules in, 103; key differences between radical teams and, 61; listed, 60; meetings of, 5–6; practices of, listed, 61; practices of, versus radical teams,

59–74; results of, versus radical teams, 18–19; speed in, versus in radical teams, 60–65

Training, 187, 191–195; integration of, with project work, 194; just-in-time, 194; start-up, 192–193; of teams versus individuals, 191–192. *See also* Kick-off sessions

Tunnel vision, 69–70

U

Uncertainty: acknowledging, 83–87, 210; exercise for assessing, 85; guidelines for assessing, 84–85; preconceived solutions and, 86–87; radical versus traditional approaches to, 62; signs of projects with, 84–87; speed and, 83–87; techniques for, 86–87

Unexpected events, learning from, 28

Unfreezing, 182

U. S. Army's after action review (AAR) process, 164, 174, 195–197

Unknown: as criterion for wicked problem, 12, 84; as project characteristic, 12; in research study projects, listed, 14. *See also* Uncertainty

Urgency, creating a sense of, 182

Utility organizations: deregulation and cost reduction problems of, 4–5, 78, 83; project definition for, 188–189; project teams of, listed, 14. *See also* Best Practice Dissemination Team; Cost Reduction Team; Leadership Development Team; Reducing Duplicate Operations Team; Staff Empowerment Team

V

Van de Ven, A. H., 29

Vesey, J. T., 94

Visibility, for stakeholders, 164

W

Warning signs. *See* Early warning signs

Waterfall model, 28, 223

Watkins, K., 127–128

Wicked problems, 11–13. *See also* Project definition; Projects

Writing Improvement Team, profile of, 14

Wycloff, K., 155